Past Masters
General Editor Keith Th

Paine

Mark Philp is Fellow and Tutor in Politics at Oriel
College, Oxford, and the author of *Godwin's Political
Justice* (1986).

Past Masters

Mark Philp

Paine

Oxford   New York

OXFORD UNIVERSITY PRESS

1989

Oxford University Press, Walton Street, Oxford OX2 6DP

Oxford New York Toronto
Delhi Bombay Calcutta Madras Karachi
Petaling Jaya Singapore Hong Kong Tokyo
Nairobi Dar es Salaam Cape Town
Melbourne Auckland

and associated companies in
Berlin Ibadan

Oxford is a trade mark of Oxford University Press

© Mark Philp 1989

First published 1989 as an Oxford University Press paperback

British Library Cataloguing in Publication Data
Philp, Mark
Paine.—(Past masters).
1. Policies. Theories of Paine, Thomas
I. Title II. Series
320.5' 1' 0924
ISBN 0–19–287666–X

Library of Congress Cataloging in Publication Data
Philp, Mark.
Paine / Mark Philp.
p. cm. Bibliography: p. Includes Index.
1. Paine, Thomas, 1737–1809. 2. Political science—History. I. Title.
320.5' 1' 0924—dc19 JC177.A4P45 1989
ISBN 0–19–287666–X

Set by Grove Graphics
Printed in Great Britain by
The Guernsey Press Co. Ltd.,
Guernsey, Channel Islands.

For my fellow travellers — Sarah, Liz,
Fanny, Jon, Joe, and Florence

Acknowledgements

My thanks go to Martin Fitzpatrick, Iain Hampsher-Monk, Alan Ryan, Sarah Turvey, David Whitley and Jean van Altena, who commented on early drafts, to Bernie Bucky for loaning me Paul Foster's *Tom Paine*, and to Henry Hardy, Thomas Webster, and Catherine Clarke at Oxford University Press for their patience.

Contents

Preface

Tom Paine was the first international revolutionary. In the last quarter of the eighteenth century, first in America, and subsequently in Britain and France, he denounced the governments of kings and aristocrats, and fought to replace them by the institutions of representative democracy. An artisan himself originally, he was an exemplary democrat who loathed the imposture, corruption, and unnatural inequalities fostered by the hereditary system, and was driven by a heartfelt conviction that ordinary men and women were capable of governing themselves in a way which would preserve liberty and security for all. He was not a particularly original political philosopher, but his analysis of contemporary society was incisive, and his prescriptions for the new order were often truly inspired.

Paine was not just a political theorist. His forte lay in his ability to turn his writings into practical weapons of radical social and political change. In this account of his work I have sought to show the integral relationship between Paine's theoretical principles and the rhetorical skills he marshalled in order to communicate these principles to his audience. In an age in which film stars become presidents and advertising agencies seek to secure 'star' status for their politician-clients, we may have become a little blasé about the capacity of an individual to communicate to a mass audience in a way which captures, shapes, and expresses its political mood. It is an indication of Paine's abilities that he could do this a century and a half before the development of modern mass media. His writing created an audience for political ideas among men and women whose reading had been limited to the Bible, the Book of Common Prayer, and *Pilgrim's Progress*. By bringing this audience into the arena of political debate, Paine directly challenged the legitimacy of the existing aristocratic and patrician orders. On these grounds he might justly have claimed that he played a major role in the development of modern democracy—even if he would have been deeply alarmed by its present condition.

The bicentennials of the American and French Revolutions and the rise of the democratic societies in Britain are sufficient to warrant renewed attention to Paine's work. But while this book follows others in the series in being an introduction to its subject, it also includes a much fuller account of Paine's political theory and rhetorical skills than can be found in most of the work on him published so far (in this respect his American writings have received much fuller treatment, particularly at the hands of Eric Foner and A. O. Aldridge). It also pays serious attention to Paine's religious writings, and attempts to show how these dovetail with his political works. The book is not offered as a substitute for Paine's own writings: I hope that those who have not read him previously will feel encouraged to do so, and that those who are already acquainted with the texts will feel inspired to return to them. I trust that both types of reader of this book will also find new reasons to respect Paine's work, and will be prompted to consider its implications for the institutions and practices of contemporary democratic societies.

Abbreviations

References to Paine's writings are to the two-volume *Life and Major Writings of Thomas Paine*, edited by Philip S. Foner (Citadel, Secaucus, N.J., 1948). References to works in Volume 1 are prefixed by I; references to Volume 2 are prefixed by II.

AA A. O. Aldridge, *Man of Reason* (Cresset, London, 1960).

AC Alfred Cobban, *The Debate on the French Revolution 1789–1800* (A. and C. Black, London, 1950).

AG Albert Goodwin, *The Friends of Liberty* (Hutchinson, London, 1979).

EB Edmund Burke, *Reflections on the Revolution in France*, edited by Conor Cruise O'Brien (Penguin, Harmondsworth, 1969).

LS Leslie Stephen, *English Thought in the Eighteenth Century*, Volume 1 (Harcourt, Brace & World Inc., London, 1962).

MB Marilyn Butler, *Burke, Paine, Godwin and the Revolution Controversy* (Cambridge University Press, Cambridge, 1984).

MC Moncur D. Conway, *The Life of Thomas Paine*, edited by H. D. Bonner, Centenary Commemoration Issue, 1809–1909 (Watts & Co., London, 1909).

PT Thomas Paine's 'My private thoughts on a future state', which is given as an appendix to his *The Age of Reason*, edited by J. M. Robertson (Watts & Co., London, 1910).

Abbreviations

RW   Raymond Williams, *Culture and Society 1780–1950* (Penguin, Harmondsworth, 1963).

ST   *State Trials*, Volume 22, edited by T. B. Howell (London, 1812–20).

Note on emphasis: all emphasis in quotations follows that of the original.

1 Life and character

A forgotten past in the Old Country, 1737–1774

Tom Paine was born in the Norfolk town of Thetford on 29 January 1737. His father was a stay-maker, his mother the daughter of a local attorney. She was 37 when they married, eleven years her husband's senior. Their religious backgrounds contrasted sharply: she was a strict Anglican, his father a Quaker. They had two children, the younger of whom, a daughter, died in infancy. Paine was educated at the local grammar school, but left school at the age of thirteen to work with his father. In his late teens he ran away to sea, and served briefly on board a privateer. Thereafter he held a succession of stay-making jobs, and at 22 married and set up his own business. Within a year his wife died and his business failed. He subsequently embarked on a career in the excise, but in 1765 was discharged for the common practice of 'stamping'—that is, failing to check a dealer's account of the taxable goods he held in stock—and was forced to resume his trade, alternating between this and occasional jobs teaching English grammar. A year later he applied for readmission to the excise; in this he was successful, and he eventually accepted a post in Lewes, Sussex. In 1771 he remarried and combined his excise duties with running a tobacco shop. While in Lewes he was an active participant in a local debating club. A contemporary described him as a Whig in political outlook. The following year he represented the excise officers in their petition for higher wages. He spent much of the winter of 1772/3 in London promoting their cause, and wrote and had printed (but not published) a pamphlet supporting their claim. Not only was the petition unsuccessful, but in his absence his

1

business fell into debt and his activities earned him the enmity of his employers. In 1774, when his business collapsed and he was forced to leave Lewes to avoid being imprisoned for debt, his employers took the opportunity to sack him for not attending to his duties. The shop and his effects were sold by public auction, and his marriage broke up shortly thereafter. He then returned to London, obtained letters of recommendation from Benjamin Franklin whom he had met during his stay in London in 1772–3, and boarded a ship for the New World. He must have been heartily sick of the Old.

Paine was 37 years old when he emigrated to America. Within two years he had launched himself on a career as an international revolutionary which was to last until his death in 1809. In the second half of his life he played a major role in the American Revolution, was outlawed in Britain, and only narrowly escaped execution during the Revolutionary Terror which gripped France in 1793–4.

Seeking an explanation of Paine's later career, many biographers have looked to the first half of Paine's life, and have attempted to identify the factors which transformed an obscure stay-maker turned excise man into a revolutionary propagandist unequalled in his day. However, the historical evidence is inadequate to the task, and Paine never sought to dispel the obscurity of his early years. It is as if he actively sought to cut himself off from his past in the Old World so as to re-create himself in the New. This is eminently understandable. His past had been little better than a prison, and he must have welcomed the chance to escape. The New World was a land of opportunity—not least the opportunity to start life afresh. Although one may question how radically people can transform themselves, one should not underestimate the catalytic effect of revolutionary struggles on those who participate in them. As in the case of many other revolutionaries, the revolution which Paine helped make may also have helped make him.

Paine in America, 1774–1787

Paine left England in October 1774, and arrived in America at the end of November. Franklin's letters of introduction brought him employment 'by several gentlemen to instruct their sons, on very advantageous terms to myself'. Moreover, 'a Printer and Bookseller here, a Robert Aitkin has lately attempted a magazine, but having little or no turn that way himself, has applied to me for assistance. He had not above 600 subscribers when I first assisted him, we have now upwards of 1500 and daily increasing' (II.1131). Paine was employed as editor of the *Pennsylvania Magazine*, but he also developed his skills as an author. He wrote a number of articles with a strong humanitarian slant on slavery, unhappy marriages, the British in India, duelling, aristocracy, and the right of the colonies to defend themselves by recourse to arms. Although they hardly justify Philip Foner's claim that Paine would be 'remembered as a significant figure in American literature, even if he had never written anything else' (I. xii), they did introduce Paine to literary and philosophical circles in Philadelphia and sharpen his literary skills. Doubtless, they were part of the preparation for *Common Sense*.

In his first year in America, Paine seems to have fallen in with the political mood of leading American radicals, whose grievances stemmed from the Stamp Act of 1765 and associated attempts to tax the colonies directly and from the Declaratory Act of 1766, according to which Parliament had full authority to make laws binding on the American colonies 'in all cases whatsoever'. The radicals attributed these measures to the scheming of Parliament and the Ministry, and suspected that they were not supported by the king. But their dual strategy of making such policies unworkable and appealing to the king for justice over the head of Parliament gave rise only to further attempts by Britain to assert her authority. The 1760s saw a succession of crises in which colonial resistance led to initial concessions which quickly gave way to renewed efforts to secure British rule. Paine arrived in America at a relatively late stage in the conflict. Twelve of the colonies had met in a Continental Congress in September and October of 1774, and new attempts at conciliation had collapsed not long after his arrival. Following clashes between British troops and American militia at Lexington and Concord in April 1775, the situation deteriorated rapidly. A second Congress, convened in May 1775, instigated another conciliatory initiative. This also failed, with the result that hostilities in the Quebec region escalated, and Congress disavowed allegiance to Parliament the following December. Yet, while the colonies denied Parliament's right to govern them directly, they did not openly challenge the sovereignty of George III. They demanded separation, but wished to retain the British monarch as head of state. Even at this late stage, few colonists were willing to champion independence and republican government publicly.

Paine wrote *Common Sense* in the autumn of 1775, and it was published on 10 January 1776. If it was not the first pamphlet to argue openly for independence and republican government, it was certainly the first to bring the arguments to the forefront of public debate. That it had this effect was in part a matter of timing, in part a consequence of the appositeness of Paine's arguments and the rhetorical skills he deployed in support of his case. *Common Sense* was successful because in it Paine showed those prepared to countenance separation that America's ills were attributable to the monarchy, not Parliament, and it was the relatively unquestioned acceptance of the necessity of monarchical government which constituted the most important remaining strand of allegiance linking the colonists to Britain. The true advocate of separation was thus forced to conclude that the colonists had no choice but to embrace republican government and reject the rule of 'the hardened, sullen-tempered Pharaoh of England for ever' (I. 25).

But *Common Sense* was successful for another reason: its attack was accessible to the common reader. Some 150,000 copies were sold (II. 1163) and even Cheetham, one of Paine's most hostile biographers, conceded that: 'Speaking a language which the colonists had felt but not thought, its popularity, terrible in its consequences to the parent country, was unexampled in the history of the press' (C 27).

Paine later wrote that he had hardly set foot in America before it 'was set on fire about my ears' (II. 1151, 1227). *Common Sense* was to fan the flames, and it launched him on his career as a revolutionary. On 4 July 1776 he saw his hopes rewarded in the Declaration of Independence, and shortly thereafter he enlisted in the Pennsylvania Flying Camp.

Paine was aide-de-camp to General Greene at Fort Lee on the Hudson when it fell to the British, and he followed the long, weary retreat to Newark and then Brunswick. The army's morale was seriously undermined by this disastrous turn of events. Washington warned Congress that his soldiers were extremely distressed and were ill prepared for the winter, and to others he expressed the fear that 'the game will be pretty well up'. Ill equipped, disheartened, and seemingly unable to stem the British advance, the continental forces appeared to be perilously close to disaster. The loss of heart was contagious. When Paine visited Philadelphia, he found the people in a deplorable, melancholy condition, 'afraid to speak and almost to think, the public presses stopped, and nothing in circulation but fears and falsehoods'. In response, working at night, 'I sat down, and in what I may call a passion of patriotism wrote the first number of the *Crisis*' (II. 1164). It was printed in the *Pennsylvania Journal* of 19 December, and tradition has it that Washington ordered it to be read to the troops on the evening of Christmas Day, as a prelude to the battle of Trenton. The opening words are Paine's most quoted lines:

5

> These are the times that try men's souls. The summer
> soldier and the sunshine patriot will, in this crisis, shrink
> from the service of their country; but he that stands it
> *now*, deserves the love and thanks of man and woman.
> Tyranny, like hell, is not easily conquered; yet we have
> this consolation with us, that the harder the conflict, the
> more glorious the triumph. [I. 50]

The first *Crisis* is an extraordinarily powerful work. Paine
writes from the heart of the conflict as a committed patriot,
and his references to marching with the army from Fort Lee
and his vivid description of the events of the retreat give
the whole work, including the more lyrical passages, an
unequivocal authenticity and force.

This piece also launched Paine's career as a public
official. His first position was that of Secretary to a Congressional Commission established to treat with Indian
groups in Pennsylvania. In April 1777 he was made
Secretary to the Congressional Committee on Foreign
Affairs, a post he held until his resignation during the Silas
Deane affair at the beginning of 1779.

The Deane affair centred on the question of whether the
supplies provided by the French government through the
mediation of Beaumarchais prior to the alliance of 1778 had
been a gift or a loan. Deane claimed that they were a loan,
and demanded a 5 per cent commission for his role in the
transaction. Paine, supporting his friend Arthur Lee,
another American commissioner in Paris, claimed that they
were a gift, and that Deane was attempting to defraud the
government. He also believed that others besides Deane
were making profits from the public offices they filled. But
the issue called for delicacy, since it was feared that if the
transactions between America and France were made
public, then the French might withdraw from the alliance.
While Paine's fervour in defending the interests of the new
republic cannot be doubted, it cannot be said that he

displayed much tact, since he used privileged information to discredit his opponent in the popular press. Although Congress did not officially condemn him for this, he was criticized and subsequently resigned his post. Rather than give up the argument, however, he continued it in the press, thereby embarrassing the French Minister further! Moreover, he wrote as if only he could save the country from the corruption which threatened it, and once he had resigned, his prose became embittered and strident. Despite his success with *Common Sense* and the *Crisis* letters, he seems simply not to have been equipped to deal with the sophisticated infighting set off by the Deane affair.

His enemies took great pleasure in his fall, and made much of the weakness of character displayed in the incident. But they overplayed their hand. Deane was discredited in March 1782 when it became clear that he was being paid to write propaganda for the British, and he fled the country. Paine learnt his lesson, though, and his subsequent forays into such controversies show a surer touch —for example, *Public Good*.

Paine was not out of public employment for long, however. He served on several Pennsylvania citizens' committees investigating profiteering, and was also elected clerk of the Assembly. It was in this capacity, in May 1780, that he read out Washington's appeal for assistance in supplying his troops:

I assure you, every idea you can form of our distresses will fall short of the reality. There is such a combination of circumstances to exhaust the patience of the soldiery that it begins at length to be worn out, and we shall see in every line of the army the most serious features of mutiny and sedition. [MC 64]

Paine responded by drawing $500 of his salary and sending it to McClenaghan, a prominent merchant, along with a plea to the wealthy business community to support the cause. He also wrote *Crisis IX*, in which he announced the establishment of a fund to aid the continental army (omitting reference to his own part in its foundation). This shows Paine at his best, attempting to rally all classes to meet the needs of the moment and burying his differences (which were considerable) with the wealthier members of the community.

By the end of September 1779 the war in the North was effectively in abeyance, the key area of operations having moved to the Carolinas (although the British still held New York). With the fall of Yorktown in October 1781 and the surrender of some 8,000 British troops, Lord North's Ministry collapsed. Peace was inevitable, and although it took more than two years to work out the details, the war was over.

Paine's devotion to the Revolution had led him to be careless in his financial dealings. He had made little or no money from his writings, and at one stage was forced to work as a clerk to supply his wants. Towards the end of the war he applied to Washington for some recompense for his services. Washington arranged with Robert Morris that he be paid a stipend to write in support of Congress's needs, something he was already doing—indeed, his insistence on Congress's right to tax directly to support its needs lends credence to his claim 'to stand first on the list of Federalists' (II. 913). He also received some money from the French Minister, Luzerne, in recognition of the service rendered to the French cause by his *Letter to the Abbé Raynal*, and was granted some land by the Indiana Company as thanks for his service in writing *Public Good*. While this smacks of Paine having become a pensioned writer, in each case there was a definite concordance of interest and conviction. Paine would doubtless have insisted on remaining his own man with his own cause—namely, the public good. It is difficult to believe that he ever wrote contrary to the state of his beliefs at the time.

After the end of the war he turned his attention to the

question of his future. He had no income and no savings, and he had repeatedly sacrificed his own interests to the cause of Independence. He wrote to Washington, telling him that unless his services were rewarded in some way, he saw no alternative but to return to Europe and attempt to make a living there. At first, Washington did nothing; and Paine's letters to his influential friends took on an increasingly badgering, resentful tone as he tried to persuade them to represent his interests to the various public authorities. His claim that he had rendered his country substantial service was just, and the response of the various states and Congress was mean enough to justify resentment. It seems, however, that he had simply made too many enemies for the post-war, conservative-dominated assemblies and Congress to wish to reward him. After some further prompting by Paine, his friends eventually persuaded Congress to award him $3,000 as back pay, New York granted him a house and land in New Rochelle (confiscated from a Tory), and Pennsylvania found him a niggardly $500. Although not wealthy, Paine was thereby comfortably provided for, and he retired from public life, devoting himself to his farm, his friends, and his scientific interests. His only subsequent excursion into political controversy was in his *Dissertations on Government* (1786), in which he defended the bank he had helped found in 1780 and supported its refusal to issue paper money without the backing of specie.

Paine remained in America until April 1787, working on a variety of schemes, including a design for a smokeless candle. But his most impressive achievement was to design a 400-foot, single-span iron bridge, originally intended for the Schuylkill river in Pennsylvania. Its great advantage over bridges with piers was that it would not be endangered by the pack-ice which clogged the river in spring. The idea of a single-span bridge was not original, but few others had thought of building such bridges of iron. Moreover, Paine's use of a criss-cross, spider's web pattern of girders was

9

entirely novel. Once again, however, he was unable to persuade the Pennsylvania Assembly. Their deliberations dragged on, with Paine growing increasingly impatient. In the end he decided to take the 13-foot model of the bridge to Europe, to see if he could obtain financial backing for its construction there. That he had also had word from his mother only confirmed his desire to return. Once again Franklin provided letters of introduction, this time to members of the French scientific community; and armed with these, Paine bid his adopted country a temporary farewell. Entirely against his expectations, it was to be more than fifteen years before he set foot on American soil again.

Paine in Europe

In Europe, Paine visited his mother, then 90, and settled a small pension on her. His plans for a bridge won respect on both sides of the Channel, but financial backing proved more elusive. He eventually found support in England; and a model of the bridge, 90 feet in span and 24 feet wide, was assembled in a field in Paddington, where it attracted many visitors and much admiration. A bridge similar to Paine's, executed by the same foundry as the model, and built under the supervision of one of his former assistants was eventually built over the Wear in County Durham. But Paine made nothing from this venture and, as in so much else, doubtless ended up substantially out of pocket.

Meanwhile he had resumed the mantle of pamphleteer. In *Prospects on the Rubicon* he warned Britain against beginning a war with France, and compared the respective strengths of the two countries. Much of the analysis rested on a now outdated mercantilism which took gold and silver holdings as the paramount indicators of national wealth. But more perplexing to modern readers in all probability is Paine's willingness to support the French monarchy. In

Prospects and in his correspondence Paine refrained from advocating republican government for either France or England. Instead, he subscribed to the view, then common in France, that the State is a union of the common people and the monarch, and that their interests are entirely harmonious. In a letter to Jefferson in February 1789 he referred to 'an internal alliance' (of Throne and people) in France, which he saw as coming to fruition and heralding a new age in French affairs: 'They are now got, or getting, into the right way, and the present reign will be more immortalised in France than any that ever preceded it' (II. 1280).

Prospects seems to support the view that Paine did not see revolution and republican government as appropriate for either country; but this interpretation is difficult to square with his other writings, particularly those on America in which he argues that monarchy is essentially an illegitimate institution. (We should bear in mind, though, that his American writings appeared in France shorn of their radical republican sentiments, with the result that he was known there as a revolutionary royalist.) *Prospects* is best read as an attempt to render service to France by warning England of the cost of aggression. Further, his subscription to existing orthodoxy in French political circles may have been more a matter of caution or courtesy than an indication of his own position. The desire to aid France is understandable, given Paine's sense of America's indebtedness to her. But it must also be said that Paine's view of the character of the masses in Europe at the time was not especially flattering:

Were governments to offer freedom to the people, or to show anxiety for that purpose, the offer would most probably be rejected . . . the desire must originate with, and proceed from the mass of the people, and when the impression becomes universal, and not before, is the most important moment for the most effectual consolidation

11

of national strength and greatness that can take place. [II. 634]

It would be entirely in keeping with the position taken in his American writings to argue that the people of Europe were simply too corrupt for republican government, and that some form of alliance between king and people was the best that could be hoped for. This interpretation also allows us to recognize *Prospects* as a transitional work between his writings maintaining that America is uniquely suited to republican government and the universal and progressive republicanism which he preaches in *The Rights of Man*.

Paine visited France in June 1787 and again in February and March 1788; and when in England, he corresponded with Jefferson in Paris, each keeping the other informed of developments in the countries in which they were living. At first he was welcomed in England by leading Whigs, who found him a useful source of information on French and American affairs; but he failed to respond to their overtures for aid in effecting a reconciliation between Britain and the New World, and relations gradually cooled. Rather surprisingly, he and Burke enjoyed each other's company, and did not seem unduly bothered by their ideological differences, Burke referred to him as 'the great American', and Paine was equally fulsome, despite warnings from Richard Price and Joseph Priestley that Burke's position was becoming increasingly unfavourable to them.

He returned to Paris in the winter of 1789/90, and wrote to Washington that he hoped to take an active part in the Revolution—'A share in two revolutions is living to some purpose' (AA 125). It is not entirely clear what he did there, since his participation in French affairs must have been hampered by his inability to speak the language. However, he was close to Lafayette and his circle, and was therefore close to the heart of the Revolution at that time. Just prior to Paine's return to England, Lafayette entrusted him with delivery of the key of the Bastille to Washington, as testimony, Paine believed, that it was the principles of the American Revolution which had brought about the downfall of the Old Regime. While in France, Paine had written to Burke on the progress of the Revolution, hoping to persuade him of its beneficial character and to allay some of the doubts aroused in England by rumours of disturbances. Like many of his contemporaries, he was shocked to hear that Burke's Speech on the Army Estimates of February 1790 denied that events in France bore any resemblance to the Glorious Revolution of 1688, accused the French of being the 'ablest architects of ruin that had hitherto existed in the world', and warned of the contagion which 'the present distemper of France' threatened. A week later Burke announced that he expected to publish a public letter justifying his attack on France. Paine reported that, 'As the attack was made in a language but little studied and less understood in France, and as everything suffers by translation, I promised some friends of the revolution in that country, that whenever Mr Burke's pamphlet came forth, I would answer it' (I. 245). It is unlikely that he needed much encouragement, since he had been collecting materials on France for some time, and had long intended to address his country of birth on the fundamentals of politics. Burke's pamphlet eventually appeared in November 1790 as *Reflections on the Revolution in France*. The pamphlet sparked off what has become known as the 'debate on France', described by Alfred Cobban as 'perhaps the last real discussion of the fundamentals of politics in this country . . .' (AC 31). More than a hundred pamphlets were eventually published, predominantly against Burke, and while many were ephemeral, some stand as major contributions to political thought (such as James Mackintosh's *Vindiciae Gallicae* and William Godwin's *Enquiry Concerning Political Justice*). As Cobban argued, 'Issues as great have been discussed in our day, but it cannot be pretended that they

13

have evoked a political discussion on the intellectual level of that inspired by the French Revolution' (AC 31). Much against Burke's intention, the debate undoubtedly spread the French 'distemper' of revolution and reform, and triggered the development of a widespread extra-parliamentary movement for political reform. Societies for the dissemination of republican and democratic political literature, such as the Society for Constitutional Information which had canvassed for reforms in the franchise in the 1770s and early 1780s, once again flourished in London and the provinces, and ensured that the attacks on Burke (and thereby on the existing political system in England) were widely circulated.

Paine's *Rights of Man*, Parts One and Two was by far the most successful, and radical of the pamphlets. The work played a major part in bringing the French Revolution home to Britain; above all, by achieving an extensive circulation—scholarly opinion gives a figure of around 100,000 copies sold in the first two years—among all classes of society, it helped stimulate a broad-based popular movement for political reform, which brought the lower orders of society into the political arena for the first time and thereby posed an unprecedented threat to the status quo. The extra-parliamentary movement was at its strongest between 1792 and 1795, when Paine was in France, but it cannot be doubted that his writings did much to prepare the ground for its emergence.

Paine left for France just before his pamphlet appeared, and once more became embroiled in revolutionary politics. Following the king's flight to Varennes and his enforced return with his family to Paris in June 1791, Paine joined Condorcet, Du Châtelet, and two others (probably including Brissot) in forming a Republican Society. On 1 July under Du Châtelet's signature, the society published a republican manifesto, which they posted on the walls of Paris (and on the door of the National Assembly), declaring that the bond between the king and the people had been broken and arguing for the abandonment of the institution of monarchy.

An office that may be filled by a person without talent or experience, an office that does not require virtue or wisdom, for its due exercise, an office which is the reward of birth, and which may consequently devolve on a madman, an imbecile or a tyrant, is, in the very nature of things an absurdity, and, whatever its ostentation, has no utility. [II.517]

There is no doubt that Paine was far ahead of most of his contemporaries at this point. There were demands for a republic from the Midi and the Cordeliers, it is true; but neither Marat nor Robespierre was prepared to advocate its formation, and Danton could only suggest a regency. Lacking the support of the leaders of the Revolution, the *de facto* republic which followed the king's flight gave way to a compromise between the king and the constituent assembly, resulting in a slightly revised constitution and a brief conservative reaction, which Paine missed by leaving for London on 9 July to attend a dinner held by the 'Friends of Liberty' to celebrate the anniversary of the fall of the Bastille.

Back in England, Paine devoted his energies to supporting the societies campaigning for parliamentary reform and to writing the second part of the *Rights of Man*, which was published in February 1792. Although his unequivocal advocacy of republican government did not command wide support in the radical societies, the pamphlet's vigorous attack on parliamentary corruption, its practical proposals rooted in a deep humanitarian concern for the poor, and its millenarian enthusiasm for the new age which was dawning won it an extraordinarily wide readership, and fanned the flames of popular discontent still further. The success of his writings, the flurry of radical publications which they encouraged, and the spread of political associations among the lower orders were increasingly vexing to Pitt and his ministers, who saw them as a threat to social order. In May the Government agreed to prosecute Paine on the grounds that Part Two was a libel on the British Constitution, and simultaneously issued a royal proclamation against seditious writings to discourage its circulation. But the machinery of British justice moved slowly. Paine was summoned for trial in June, but the case was deferred until November. The delay left Paine in his element. He was now relatively immune from immediate government action, and he had a dual cause to defend—his own right to publish and the public's right to read. He wrote public letters to the Attorney-General and the Home Secretary, denouncing the Government's attempt to suppress discussion and ridiculing the royal proclamation for trying to tell people what they should believe. But his most striking piece, referred to by many as a third part to the *Rights of Man*, was his *Letter Addressed to the Addressers on the Late Proclamation*, which flatly denied the legitimacy of Britain's existing political system and called for the establishment of a national convention to frame a popular government for Britain. It was tantamount to an open call for revolution, and it helped to prepare the ground for the radical societies' attempts to call a convention at the end of 1793 and in the spring of 1794. These attempts led to the imprisonment of the leaders of the Society for Constitutional Information and the London Corresponding Society and to their trial for treason late in 1794.

None of Paine's writings in the summer of 1792 seemed likely to strengthen his chances of acquittal, and it is doubtful (once the trial had been postponed) whether he intended to appear in court. He left England, delayed but not arrested by ministerial agents, in September 1792. If there had been any doubt as to the outcome of his trial, the letter he wrote to the Attorney-General late in September was enough to make a guilty verdict a foregone conclusion:

The time, Sir, is becoming too serious to play with Court prosecutions, and sport with national rights. The terrible examples that have taken place here upon men who, less than a year ago, thought themselves as secure as any prosecuting judge, jury, or attorney general can do now in England, ought to have some weight with men in your situation. [II. 512]

The jury found him guilty, without even retiring or bothering to hear the Attorney-General's reply to the defending attorney's plea. He was outlawed; and throughout Britain, at the instigation of loyalist associations established with the encouragement of the Government, Paine was burnt in effigy.

In France, Paine had become something of a national hero. Conway claims, with uncharacteristic hyperbole, that Lanthenas's translation of the *Rights of Man* and Sharpe's engraving of its author could be found in every home. Following the fall of the monarchy in August 1792, the National Assembly bestowed French citizenship on a number of 'friends of France', including Paine (along with his countrymen Washington, Madison, and Hamilton), and in the subsequent elections to the National Convention he was chosen as a representative by the electoral assemblies of four *départements*. He accepted the seat of Pays de Calais, returned to France on 15 September, and after a number of ceremonies and 'rather fatigued with the kissing' (AA 172), he took his place in the National Convention. The following day the monarchy was abolished. France was now a republic.

Surprisingly, Paine seems to have had no qualms about returning to France. His inability to speak the language, his past association with Lafayette, and his ignorance of the complex social and political forces unleashed by events in his year's absence did not daunt him. His willingness to assist in the formation of the new republic despite these drawbacks smacks of presumption. In all probability he was still infected with the enthusiasm he had generated and shared in England, and was still reeling from the homage paid him, first by the English Crown and its ministers and subsequently by the French people. We should recognize, however, that Paine's analysis of revolution as a process of enlightenment did not prepare him well for understanding the complex dynamic of social forces which ebbed and flowed beneath the surface of events in France. It is clear that he was frequently out of his depth during his stay there. Of course, much the same could be said of most of his contemporaries. The French Revolution was a convulsive process which few contemporary men or women mastered, either practically or intellectually.

Paine served faithfully on the Convention's Committee on the Constitution, and dutifully attended the Convention. Nevertheless, he kept a reasonably low profile—until the debate on the trial and sentencing of Louis. Although Paine defended the right of the Convention to try the king, he argued that his life should be spared, and suggested detention until the end of the war, followed by banishment to America. He argued for Louis's life on grounds of expediency, as a matter of respect for the United States which remained in his debt, and as a matter of principle—to destroy the institution was both necessary and just, whereas to destroy the individual was neither. Once the death sentence had been passed, the debate moved on to the question of reprieve. Paine wrote his opinion, *Should Louis XVI be Respited*, and stood beside the Secretary of the Convention, Bancal, as it was read in translation. Marat interrupted, initially to deny that Paine had a right to vote since he was a Quaker, later to insist with Thuriot that the translation was defective, and finally to deny Paine's right to speak because of his Quaker background.

Paine's defence of Louis was a brave, principled action, one which earned him the lasting suspicion of the Jacobins.

His fortunes declined from this point forward. The Committee on the Constitution on which he and Condorcet had spent so much time reported to the Convention in February, but discussion was repeatedly deferred at Montagnard insistence, and when the opening Declaration was introduced for discussion, it was savaged by Robespierre for its failure to pay due homage to the Supreme Being. The remainder of the document was referred to a Jacobin-dominated committee which produced a new Constitution in June. This was speedily ratified by referendum, and was then shelved for the duration of the war. In the end it was never put into practice.

Paine further alienated the Jacobins by allowing himself to be be dragged, irrelevantly, into Marat's trial, and by testifying on General Francisco Miranda's behalf when the General was tried for treason over the rout of French troops in Holland in the Dumouriez campaign. At each step his behaviour only served to confirm his enemies' view that his sympathies lay with the increasingly weak and discredited Girondins. By the summer of 1793 the Girondins were broken. Their leading members, including many of Paine's friends, were suspended from the Convention and imprisoned in June, and were then executed in October. Others, like Condorcet, went into hiding. By then Paine's confidence had deserted him. In April of that year he had written to Jefferson admitting that there was no longer any prospect of a general European revolution (II. 1331), and in May he had written to Danton expressing his extreme concern that 'the distractions, jealousies, discontents and uneasiness that reign among us . . . will bring ruin and disgrace upon the Republic'. Clearly depressed and fearful for his own safety, he started to drink excessively.

He was eventually arrested and imprisoned in the Palais de Luxembourg on 28 December 1793. It had been clear for some time that he would be arrested—although he was never officially charged with an offence. He had been

19

denounced in the Convention by Amar in October and by Barrère and de l'Oise in December—on both occasions being associated with the Girondins. Moreover, his chances of being overlooked were slight. Yet he made no effort to escape or to go into hiding. Although his inability to speak the language and his lack of a passport would have made escape difficult, it seems very much as if he resigned himself to his fate. Once he had conquered his despair, he ignored events as far as possible, devoting his time to his friends and to writing what he believed would be his last work, *The Age of Reason*. Writing later to Samuel Adams, he recalled:

> My friends were falling as fast as the guillotine could cut their heads off, and as I expected every day the same fate, I resolved to begin my work. I appeared to myself to be on my death bed, for death was on every side of me, and I had no time to lose. . . . I had not finished the first part of the work more than six hours before I was arrested and taken to prison. [II. 1436; letter dated 1 January 1803]

The precise grounds for Paine's arrest are as unclear as the reasons for his survival. Some time after, shortly before his own fall, Robespierre wrote a note demanding that Paine be 'decreed of accusation for the interests of America as much as of France' (MC 88). Conway has argued that Paine was a victim of a conspiracy by Gouverneur Morris, the American Minister in France, whose enmity went back to the Silas Deane affair. Aldridge's interpretation of Morris's role is more sympathetic, but is not entirely convincing (AA 201–4). It seems likely that Paine would have been released if America had been more actively concerned for his welfare. Moreover, Robespierre's suggestion that Paine be brought to trial—meaning, in effect, brought up for execution—'in the interests of America', suggests that Morris had taken some positive steps to denounce him.

Given Robespierre's note, it is a mystery how Paine eluded the guillotine. He always attributed his survival to the fact that the mark made on the doors of condemned prisoners was inadvertently put on the inside of his door and was thus concealed when the executioners came for their cargo that night. But even if this story is fanciful it remains true that he was lucky to escape with his life: he became seriously ill while in prison, and it took more than a year for him to recover fully.

Characteristically, Paine ascribed his survival to the guiding hand of Providence. He assigned his release, on 4 November 1794, some three months after Robespierre's fall, to the replacement of Morris by James Monroe, who not only pressed Paine's case with the authorities, but took him into his home while he slowly recovered his health. Once released, Paine was reclaimed by the National Convention, and was reinstated with full honours. Despite his poor health he resumed work on Part Two of the *Age of Reason*. He also contributed to the debate on the new constitution in July 1795, first with his *Dissertation on the First Principles of Government*—essentially an epitome of the *Rights of Man*—and subsequently with *The Constitution of 1795*, in which he argued powerfully, if without effect, for the replacement of the proposed property-based franchise by universal suffrage. Despite his experiences, Paine never lost faith in the virtue of the people.

Once out of prison, Paine's resentment of America's apparent desertion of him festered; and despite Monroe's best efforts to persuade him to drop the matter, he became increasingly convinced that Washington had sacrificed him to other interests. He eventually wrote, and had published in America, *The Letter to George Washington*, in which he accused the president of betraying his friendship and leaving him to die. Predictably, the letter was seen by many as an unseemly attack on the country's senior statesman, and it did Paine much harm in America.

By the end of 1796 Paine had recovered his health, and he promptly produced two of his most innovative and important pamphlets: *The Decline and Fall of the English System of Finance* and *Agrarian Justice* (see chapter 3). *Decline and Fall* and his defence of the Directory's purging of royalist elements in the Council of Five Hundred on 18 Fructidor (4 September 1797) confirmed Paine's good standing with the French authorities. Following Jay's treaty with England and the related seizure of three hundred American merchant ships by France in June 1797, relations between America and France became increasingly strained, and Paine was able (and keen) to act as an informal ambassador for American citizens and interests in France. He also used his standing to encourage the Directory, and subsequently Napoleon, to attempt the invasion of England. He believed that the vast majority of the population would greet the invading force as an army of liberation, and that a revolution could be achieved with minimal bloodshed. Paine did not see republics as having *carte blanche* to bring revolutions to subject peoples. Rather, he advocated the invasion of Britain as a legitimate act of war and as a reprisal for Britain's attempts to invade France.

Paine's good opinion of the Directory gradually eroded as the republic slid rapidly towards its end. Moreover, the Directory became similarly disenchanted with Paine. While this was partly due to the limited, undeclared war between America and France during 1798–1800, it also stemmed from Paine's own indiscretions in his friendships and activities. After 1797, however, his concerns focused increasingly on American affairs, an indication that he saw himself as simply killing time in France, and now longed to return home.

Paine had tried to return to his adopted country on several occasions, but had been denied permission while he was a member of the Convention, and had feared returning after its dissolution because of the risk of being seized by a British warship. He eventually boarded an American merchant ship during the Amiens peace of 1802–3, arriving in America on 1 November 1802. He was now 65 years old.

The new America

Paine's last years in America were not happy ones. He was an easy target for the anti-Jacobin campaign conducted by the Federalist opposition to Jefferson's administration. Although he inspired enmity in his own right (by his deism and his open support of the French Revolution), his friendship with Jefferson made him a suitable candidate for character assassination twice over. Jefferson behaved well to Paine. He was free with his hospitality (to the Federalists' indignation), and Paine stayed with him in Washington, probably deriving more pleasure from this than from anything else in this difficult, turbulent period of his life. But he was not offered public office—Jefferson had good reason for believing that he was not sufficiently discreet for such responsibilities.

Paine's health began to deteriorate after July 1806, when he suffered an attack of apoplexy. He recovered enough to write a good deal of polemic, as well as another part of the *Age of Reason* and some advice on naval strategy. But his work was increasingly interrupted by bouts of illness, and he died in June 1809, having refused to recant his religious opinions.

A question of character

Paine may have been justified in believing that Providence had saved his body for a natural death. But Providence proved unequal to the task of shielding his character from assassins, both in his lifetime and subsequently. He emerged relatively unscathed from the American Revolution, but was not so fortunate later on. The British government opened the campaign against his reputation by commissioning a suitably nasty piece of work by George Chalmers, under the pseudonym Francis Oldys. Oldys was succeeded by James Cheetham, a past associate of Paine's, who in 1809 was rewarded by the Federalists for an equally prejudiced, scurrilous biography. Paine was depicted as a drunkard who was filthy in his personal habits, soiled his bed when drunk, and had to be bathed forcibly. Friends and supporters of Paine subsequently responded to both accounts; but it was not until Conway's painstaking work published in 1892 that Paine's reputation made a substantial recovery.

Yet this concern with Paine's character and reputation is largely beside the point. It is true that Paine drank—his partiality being for brandy. On occasion he seems to have got drunk, particularly in the summer of 1793, probably when stranded in France after his release from prison, and probably during the last years of his life. It is also true that he was not particularly concerned about his personal appearance, and that he was incontinent for periods after his stroke. But the question of whether there is anything of merit in his political theory or theology cannot be determined by the level of alcohol in his bloodstream or by how frequently he washed his clothes. The one area in which this kind of detail might be important, even though it cannot be recovered completely by the historian—after all, it is possible to disagree in our judgements of character of people still living—is that of Paine's integrity. But on this issue, there is no doubt that Paine must command respect. It is true that on occasion he acted arrogantly, that he was proud of his fame (some would say conceited), that persecution made him fearful and sometimes boastful, that he responded to the enmity of others in kind, and so on—in short, that he was a flawed human being, who, like most of us, treated his friends better than his enemies and sometimes confused the demands of reason with the dictates of his own passions and prejudices. But there is no evidence that he ever acted falsely to his friends, or that he was cruel without regret or malicious without thought or reason, or that he lied or cheated to serve his own selfish ends. Towards the end of his life, feeling deserted by his adopted country and his former friends, he fell to boasting of his remaining friends in high places (in circumstances which did no one any good), but it is difficult not to sympathize. More to the point, there is nothing to suggest that he prostituted his pen for ends which he personally rejected or that he was motivated by personal ambition in what he wrote. He was generous to the causes he served, giving his time, energy, and money to the continental cause, the radical societies in Britain, and the French republic. And in each case he was prepared to risk his life. As it turned out, this was not particularly prudent behaviour; but it was certainly not self-serving. There is little room for doubt that Paine held to his political principles, that he saw no better life on earth than that devoted to the public good and the science of nature, and that if we seek a deeper motive, we are best advised to look to his belief in a future state or afterlife.

It remains the case, however, that the obsession with Paine's character is largely misplaced, since at best it can shed only limited light on his arguments and his significance as a political theorist. These have an independent weight, and deserve close scrutiny; and it is to this task that we now turn.

2 America

In *Common Sense* Paine argues for American independence from Britain and for the founding of a republican government for the colonies. Drawing on English and colonial traditions of opposition political thought, he savages claims for the legitimacy of English rule and arguments for reconciliation, and shows how the colonies might provide their own government. *Common Sense* is an onslaught on the old order and the vices it supports and a clarion call to the virtue of citizens upon whose shoulders the hopes of the New World rest.

The old order

Paine begins his attack by distinguishing between society and government:

> Society is produced by our wants and government by our wickedness; the former promotes our happiness *positively* by uniting our affections, the latter *negatively* by restraining our vices. . . . Society is in every state a blessing, but government, even in its best state, is but a necessary evil; in its worst state [it is] an intolerable one. . . . Government, like dress, is the badge of lost innocence; the palaces of kings are built upon the ruins of the bowers of paradise. For were the impulses of conscience clear, uniform and irresistibly obeyed, men would need no other law giver. [I. 4–5]

He sees the state of nature as a social state in which natural liberty flourishes, and government, the 'badge of lost innocence', as a common power set over society. This power derives from consent and has a legitimate function—

namely, the exercise of sovereignty in defence of the public good. But unless restrained, government becomes tyrannical and threatens the liberty and security of those whom it was established to protect. Good governments pursue the common good; tyrants pursue their own interests. Free political societies are sanctioned by reason and nature; but, given human frailty, they are fragile polities. They rest on the wisdom and virtues of their citizens and on the social and political institutions which wisdom contrives and virtue sustains; but they are beset by myriad forces of corruption.

The Country Party and Commonwealthman traditions of eighteenth-century political thought held that the liberty and security of Englishmen rested on the balance in the English constitution between the prerogative powers of the Crown and the interests of the people as represented in Parliament. Were the Crown to find ways to suborn the representatives of the people to its personal interest, the liberty of the nation would be lost. In fact, the Crown had considerable resources for corrupting Parliament: it could offer pensions, and it controlled appointments to the Court and the Army. Its position was strengthened by the flourishing of commerce, which undermined civic virtue by encouraging men to consider only their self-interest. In the more classically influenced republican theories of Machiavelli and Rousseau, civic virtue and liberty required an austere civic life in which citizens identified their own good wholly with the common good. In the eighteenth century, however, many writers were prepared to advance a less austere (and less consistent) republicanism, and welcomed commerce as a stimulant to leisure, culture, the arts, and the development of civilization. Yet these writers retained the belief that the security of a republic and the liberty of its citizens required the existence of a body of men whose independent means would enable them to resist the corrupting influence of the Crown and to ensure that Parliament remain true to the interests of the people as a whole. This preference for an independent gentry meant that few republicans countenanced extending the franchise to the common people. Republican government was free government because it preserved liberty, but it was not necessarily democratic government. Most republicans believed that democracy would mean rule by the mob—that is, by people who lacked the education, culture, and financial independence necessary for political activity. Instead, they saw the balance between king and Parliament as a means of restraining both individual and collective forms of tyranny. Drawing on Aristotelian and Polybian ideas of a mixed Constitution and on the works of Machiavelli, Harrington, and Montesquieu, they interpreted the English Constitution as providing a division of powers between the various organs of government and a mixture of rule by the one, the few, and the many (monarchy, aristocracy, and democracy). Court apologists held that the powers and orders of government were interdependent, and that the exercise of influence by the Crown was an integral component of the balanced Constitution. Their Country Party opponents insisted on the independence of the various organs, and saw Crown influence as necessarily corrupt. But both groups accepted the premiss that a mixed Constitution is less likely than pure forms (monarchy, aristocracy, or democracy) to degenerate into excess and tyranny, for it is the fragmentation of power and the clash of the various interests in the state which ensure liberty. When one organ of government is able to seduce another to support its personal ambitions, then the balance is destroyed, the Constitution is in danger, and liberty is lost.

Paine's Revolution writings are deeply indebted to this tradition. He fears that the security and liberty of the people will be engulfed by tyranny. The doctrines of mixed government and the separation of powers inform his attack on the parlous state of the English polity, and, like many of his new countrymen, he insists that the forces of corruption in

England are so rampant that the flame of liberty which she has long preserved is on the point of extinction. *Common Sense* and Paine's other Revolution writings are peppered with acerbic denunciations of the English Constitution and the machinations of the king and his ministers, and give ample confirmation of his indebtedness to this tradition of opposition thought. The Crown is 'the overbearing part in the English Constitution' (I. 8); the 'monarchy has poison-ed the Republic; the crown has engrossed the Commons' (I. 16); the king is a 'miserable tyrant' (I. 105); the Court is pilloried as 'corrupt and faithless' (I. 44), a repository for 'extravagance and rapaciousness' (I. 175), 'easy virtue' (I. 60), and 'dangling parasites' (I. 62); the ministry is 'per-fidious' (ibid.), 'a detestable junto' (I. 24) which knows 'no other influence than corruption' (I. 148), and which is con-spiring to the annexation and despoiling of America; Parlia-ment is 'pensioned' (I. 118), its business being bribery and corruption; and the country is ready to 'add the final vice to national corruption' (I. 210)—that is, to surrender itself to tyranny. In short, the English polity comprises a 'foolish tyrant, a debauched court, a trafficking legislature, (and) a blinded people' (I. 66). Paine also shares the view that England's dealings with America confirm that the Ministry has subverted Parliament and is bent on the annexation and pillage of the colonies to support its expenses and military ambitions. Nor is he alone in believing that what is at stake is not just the liberty of Americans but the flame of liberty itself:

> Every spot of the world is overrun with oppression. Freedom hath been hunted round the globe. Asia and Africa have long expelled her. Europe regards her like a stranger, and England hath given her warning to depart. O! receive the fugitive, and prepare in time an asylum for mankind. [I. 31]

Yet, while he shares the characteristic thrust and

29

framework of opposition thought, Paine's account is un-
orthodox. He breaks with the tradition by ignoring arguments about the existence of an ancient Constitution in
England; he denies that monarchy can ever be legitimate;
and he equates republican government with democratic
government. He also challenges the doctrines of mixed
government and the balanced Constitution. The English
Constitution is composed of the 'base remains of two
ancient tyrannies (monarchy and aristocracy) compounded
with new Republican materials' (I. 7). The House of Commons is the sole republican element: England's freedom rests
entirely on 'the liberty of choosing an House of Commons
out of their own body' and on the virtue of its citizens (I. 16).
Paine is able simultaneously to utilize and to transcend this
tradition of thought, primarily because he distinguishes between the political orders and possibilities of the Old and the
New World. England's political system is corrupt to the point
of being almost beyond redemption, and her tyranny now
threatens the liberty of the American colonies. Yet, while the
threat is great, so too are the opportunities:

> The present time . . . is that peculiar time which never
> happens to a nation but once, viz. the time of forming
> itself into a government. Most nations have let slip the
> opportunity, and by that means have been compelled to
> receive laws from their conquerors, instead of making
> laws for themselves. First they had a king, and then a
> form of government; whereas the articles or charter of a
> government should be formed first, and men delegated to
> execute them afterwards [I. 36–7]

The colonies are in an exceptional position in that
Providence has granted them the opportunity to build a
government from first principles. If they act wisely, they
can provide the world with a 'sanctuary for the persecuted',
a 'refuge for liberty', and an 'asylum for mankind' (I. 21,
31). To be successful they must found their government on

the equality of mankind and 'the simple voice of reason and nature'.

Common Sense opens by arguing that only republican government can satisfy these conditions. Monarchy is supported by neither reason nor the Scriptures. Monarchies have laid 'the world in blood and ashes' (I. 16); they inevitably tend to corruption and tyranny; they are founded on conquest, usurpation, force, and fraud; and the associated principle of hereditary succession is anathema to all rational men, since it 'opens the door to the *foolish*, the *wicked*, and the *improper*, [and] has in it the nature of oppression' (I. 15). Moreover, the Scriptures show that a people granted the opportunity to found a republic and live as equals sins against God if it establishes a monarchy: 'Tis a form of government which the word of God bears testimony against, and blood will attend it' (I. 16). The old order is unnatural, irrational, and corrupt, and stands condemned in the sight of God. It cannot supply a model for the people of America, for whom Providence has ordained a special destiny.

The new republic

The inhabitants of heaven long to see the ark finished in which all the liberty and true religion in the world are to be deposited. [II. 93]

For Paine, the time for the new republic was at hand: independence is demanded by prudence, necessity, natural right, and our duty to our one true Sovereign. Indeed, America is already effectively self-governing; but its autonomy rests entirely on the virtue of its people, since the country lacks the necessary political infrastructure. Paine regards the present state of affairs as truly alarming, since the country is 'without law, without government, without any other mode of power than what is founded on,

31

and granted by, courtesy'. Moreover, it is 'held together by an unexampled occurrence of sentiment' which is extremely vulnerable to subversion. He says: 'Our present condition is, Legislation without law; wisdom without a plan; a constitution without a name; and, what is strangely astonishing, perfect independence contending for dependence' (I. 43)

To guide the American people in this crisis, Paine offers a parable. He asks his readers to imagine 'a small number of persons, settled in some sequestered part of the earth, unconnected with the rest' (I. 5). Society will be their first thought, for without co-operation they will perish. Necessity brings them together, unites them in a common cause, and ensures that they act justly. As their situation improves, however, they 'begin to relax in their duty and attachment to each other' and it becomes clear that some form of government is required to 'supply the defect in moral virtue'. The people begin by meeting under 'some convenient tree' to determine rules to regulate their conduct; but as the population of the colony increases (as it always does under free government), the need for some form of representative government becomes apparent. Frequent elections will ensure that 'the *elected* will never form to themselves an interest separate from the *electors* . . . [and] this frequent interchange will establish a common interest with every part of the community . . . and on this (not on the unmeaning name of king,) depends *the strength of government and the happiness of the governed*' (I. 6).

The meaning of the parable is plain. Paine emphasizes America's geographical separation from Europe, the fact that its inhabitants have fled to it for sanctuary and have no real connection with their former countries, and the extent to which America has developed along its own path and has gained a sense of its own identity and unity. With the rupture in its relations with Britain, it is left with 'no law but moderated passions; no other civil power than an honest mob; and no other protection than the temporary attachment of one man to another' (I. 81). While the natural ties of duty and attachment are not strong enough to allow the colony to subsist without government for long, the people's natural sentiments, fellow-feeling, and virtue remain sufficiently uncorrupted for them to form a representative republic. Only by doing so can America secure the public good and avoid the corruption and degeneration which have affected the European states. But the opportunity must be seized, for 'It may not always happen that our soldiers are citizens, and the multitude a body of reasonable men; virtue is not hereditary, neither is it perpetual'. America's future happiness can be assured only if she establishes a government for herself on first principles. If she does so, virtue can be preserved; if not, the cause and the country are lost (I. 45).

The basic principles enshrined in Paine's parable—political equality, minimal and representative government, the integrative role of social affection and commerce, and the requirement that government pursue the common good—underpin his analysis of the appropriate form of government for the colonies. Because the colonies are too extensive and too populous to allow a convention of the whole people, he proposes a continental conference, with representatives from the existing Continental Congress, from each State Assembly or Provincial Convention, and from the people at large, chosen by popular vote. This conference will design the continental charter, or Constitution. Its task will be to devise a mode of government that contains 'the greatest sum of individual happiness, with the least national expense' (I. 29). Paine sees the element of popular involvement in the construction of the Constitution as tantamount to a social contract: 'a charter is to be understood as a solemn bond of obligation, which the whole enter into, to support the right of every separate part, whether of religion, professional freedom or property'

(I. 37). He believes that a freely formed Constitution is the only basis for legitimate government, and hence his sharp distinction between countries with Constitutions and those, like Britain, where 'there is *no* Constitution, but only *a temporary form of government*' (I. 85).

Paine says little about the form which the Constitution should take. In *Common Sense* he suggests that the Continental Congress be unicameral, that it elect a president from among its members (with the presidency rotating among the thirteen states), and that, 'in order that nothing may pass into a law but what is just, not less than three-fifths of the Congress' be taken as a majority (I. 28). He also insists on the importance of ensuring a large, equal representation. In his *A Serious Address to the People of Pennsylvania* (1778) he defends the radical State Constitution proposed by the Convention, and makes a powerful case for extending suffrage beyond the customary property-based franchise to include all independent men, whether rich or poor, as a matter of right. 'Wherever I use the words *freedoms* or *rights*, I desire to be understood to mean a perfect equality of them. Let the rich man enjoy his riches, and the poor man comfort himself in his poverty. But the floor of freedom is as level as water' (II. 287). Only men who freely subordinate themselves to another or to the public and who thereby consent to serve another should lack a vote. Moreover, they should 'repossess their full share of freedom' the instant 'they assume their original independent character of a man and encounter the world in their own persons' (I. 287).

A legitimate government can derive only from a Constitution founded by popular consent; and frequent popular elections both ensure that those elected remain faithful to their task and preserve citizens from arbitrary power. The populist, democratic thrust of Paine's position is unequivocal—so much so that on at least one occasion he speaks in Rousseau-like terms of the will of the people as the true sovereign: 'We have hitherto confounded two distinct things together, which ought to be kept separate; I mean, *the sovereignty of the United States*, and the *delegated representation of that sovereignty in Congress* . . . it may happen that the character of the latter falls short of the former' (II. 169). Sovereignty rests with the people as a collective body, not with their representatives.

Paine's concern with the *'sovereignty of the United States'* was not simply populist rhetoric. His demands for minimal government and his claim that government is always an evil notwithstanding, he believed that America required strong continent-wide government if it was to unite the country. In *Common Sense* he demonstrates little concern with the States' rights against Congress, suggesting that the business of the State assemblies will be 'wholly domestic, and subject to the authority of the Continental Congress' (I. 28). Moreover, his proposal that the people be directly represented at the Constitutional Convention and his associated denial of the right of State assemblies to elect delegates show that he has no time for pretensions of State sovereignty as against national sovereignty. For Paine, 'our strength is continental, not provincial' (I.29); and the problem is that 'the continental belt is too loosely buckled' (I. 44). 'The union of America is the foundation-stone of her independence' (I. 204); and when we reflect on the way the Union has been able to sustain and win the war for independence' (when individually the States would have been crushed), we must 'be strongly impressed with the advantage, as well as the necessity of strengthening that happy union which has been our salvation, and without which we would have been a ruined people' (I. 232).

We have no other national sovereignty than as United States. . . . Sovereignty must have power to protect all the parts that comprise it; and as UNITED STATES we are equal to the importance of the title, but otherwise we are not.

35

. . . Our citizenship in the United States is our national character. Our citizenship in any particular state is only our local distinction. [I. 234]

Despite Paine's democratic leanings, his comments on the new Constitution fall short of both the letter and the spirit of his parable. The Constitution is not to be ratified by popular vote; nor is universal suffrage insisted upon. Paine does not show why delegation and representation, both of which are anathema to Rousseau, are acceptable substitutes for direct participation. Moreover, his treatment of consent is somewhat cavalier—voting in an election of representatives to a Constitutional Convention is taken as fully contractual consent to whatever the Convention sees fit to prescribe—and his demands for national sovereignty are made with scant regard for contractarian principles—national sovereignty is demanded by the public good, and neither individuals nor states have rights against this end.

Paine's arguments on these issues are either weak or nonexistent, in part because of his self-appointed role as a polemicist for the Revolution—polemics are not treatises of political theory—and in part because he makes extensive use of the language and traditions of argument of both natural-rights thinkers and republican political theorists, which are, if not necessarily contradictory, at least uneasy bedfellows.

Liberty and the public good

There seems little doubt of the extent of Paine's commitment to a rights-based political theory. The entire point of government is to preserve the rights which individuals have in the state of nature—that is, their rights to liberty, security, and freedom of conscience (II. 54). His account of constitutional principles and the American Constitution is motivated by his belief that the rule of law and hence the equal liberty of all must be maintained. His comments on commerce go even further, by suggesting that a free society is one which allows every individual the liberty to exercise his or her natural abilities or talents in the pursuit of his or her own interests. In this he looks very much like a modern libertarian arguing for minimal government and the free operation of the market economy.

Yet Paine is also committed to a form of republicanism which is incompatible with libertarianism because of the overriding importance it assigns to civic virtue and the common good. Inded, his distinction between society and government, which seems so much a part of the natural-rights tradition, can also be interpreted as a distinction between a society in which people are so united by affections, feelings, social sentiment, reciprocal obligations, and a sense of natural duty that they disinterestedly pursue the common good and a society in which these bonds have become so loose that government must step in to encourage the people where possible, and coerce them where necessary, to consider the interests of the whole. While it is unrealistic to hope that civic virtue will be so widespread that all will willingly pursue the public good, a society in which most citizens lack such virtue will be incapable of sustaining republican government. For such government relies on most citizens having some capacity for placing the public good above their individual interests, while recognizing that not everyone has this capacity, and that even those who do sometimes stray from the true path of disinterestedness. Paine's denunciation of parties and factions in government confirms his commitment to a substantive conception of the common good. Parties and factions subvert government by using it to further their own particular interests, irrespective of the consequences for others. For Paine, as for other republican thinkers, a republic can flourish only when most citizens are sufficiently virtuous and public-spirited to sacrifice their own interests for the good of the community.

The tension between this view and natural-rights theories is obvious: a nation of individuals who stand on their rights and pursue their selfish interests will be incapable of sharing a conception of the common good, and therefore incapable of civic virtue. Yet Paine's commitment to the republican vision is unequivocal. He believes that republican government is objectively in the interests of all the people, that the rational and the virtuous will recognize this, and that those who do not must be encouraged to do so. He writes: 'That in which every man is interested, is every man's duty to support. And any burden which falls equally on all men, and from which every man is to receive equal benefit, is consistent with the most perfect idea of liberty' (I. 127). In other words, we do not infringe a person's freedom if we impose burdens which, were he to reason correctly, he would recognize as his just share of the cost of providing something from which he will benefit. Government, it seems, may force men to be free!

> Where men have not public spirit to render themselves serviceable, it ought to be the study of government to draw the best use possible from their vices. When the governing passion of any man, or set of men, is once known, the method of managing them is made easy; for even misers, whom no public virtue can impress, would become generous, could a heavy tax be laid upon covetousness. [I. 98]

This does not sound like minimal government; nor does it put much of a premium on the rights of individuals against the whole. Liberty is understood less as the free exercise of natural rights and more as collective self-government and the pursuit of the public good.

Paine expends a good deal of effort trying to show his readers that their real interests lie in the public good, in the hope that they will freely promote it. But he does not believe that compliance with the public good need be, or should be, based on the motive of interest. There are higher motives without which the new republic cannot survive.

> Though in matters of bounden duty and reciprocal affection, it is rather a degeneracy from the honesty and ardour of the heart to admit any thing selfish to partake in the government of our conduct, yet in cases where our duty, our affections, and our interests coincide, it may be of some use to observe their union. [I. 205]

But, even if it is of some use to observe their union, we should not mistake 'a cold matter of interest' for the beginning and end of our duty and happiness! The distinction between people's interests and their bounden duties and affections confirms Paine's commitment to the republican view that society is not simply a sphere for the pursuit of private interests. It is only in society that the higher human capacities for social affection, sentiment, civilization, the pursuit of knowledge, disinterested benevolence, and virtue become possible; and only when these capacities flourish do people recognize that their individual good lies in the common good. A republic cannot be formed where people are corrupted by luxury, suborned by titles and honours, and driven by the baser human passions of lust, avarice, pride, and egoism; hence the urgency of Paine's call for independence: 'Virtue is not hereditary, neither is it perpetual' (I. 45). If America remains under the English monarchy, her virtue will inevitably be corrupted. That monarchies corrupt their people whereas good governments reinforce their citizens' virtues helps to explain why individual rights do not necessarily clash with the imperious demands of the public good. Under good government we will come to want to do what we have a duty to do. Although Paine does not develop this point, he gives three reasons for thinking that in practice Americans will recognize that their duty and their interest coincide. The way he addresses his audience reflects his belief that a sufficiently strong bond of common sentiment exists among Americans to support republican institutions. He gives a general argument about the integrative effects of commerce. He also makes a series of claims about the support which reason lends to republican institutions, suggesting that reason itself is capable of generating an identity of individual and public good.

Common Sense

Common Sense is an apt title for Paine's call for independence, for common sense is the general sense of mankind or of a community, and denotes the common or normal understanding without which a person is deemed foolish, insane, or perverse. It is what we unquestioningly know to be true—what we take for granted about the world in which we live and what we share with others in that world. 'Common sense' is not a substitute term for reason and rationality, for the word 'sense' has connotations of sentiment and feeling, as well as reasonableness. Appeals to common sense are not simply cognitive; they are appeals to 'those feelings without which we should be incapable of discharging the duties of life or enjoying the felicities of it' (I. 23). Common sense is a kind of second nature. To fail to grasp what a people take as common sense is to be a stranger among them and a potential threat to their mores and to their social order.

Yet, because common sense is rooted in feeling and sentiment, it is usually poorly articulated, and up to a point is open to interpretation and change. Appeals to common sense are often appeals to a particular interpretation of what a group shares in common. Under certain conditions such an appeal can lead to quite dramatic shifts in patterns of belief and action as the interpretation moves certain

elements of a group's inchoate patterns of belief and action
to the centre of its self-understanding while marginalizing
others. In *Common Sense* Paine seeks to undermine his
readers' common sense of the naturalness of their subjection to Britain and to replace it with a sense of the necessity
of independence. He presents his audience with 'simple
facts, plain arguments, and common sense'; he asks its
members to put aside 'prejudice and prepossession' in
favour of reason and natural feeling; and he appeals to his
reader to 'put on . . . the true character of a man, and
generously enlarge his views beyond the present day' (I. 17).
Paine's reference to 'the true character of a man' is inten-
tionally double-edged. He flatters his audience with the
ideal of a rational, just, unprejudiced observer who judges
impartially; but he then goes on to use a variety of images,
allusions, metaphors, and similes designed to elicit the
strongest, deepest feeling among his largely male audience
by speaking to them in their various capacities of husband,
father, son, lover, and friend. It is this 'common sense'
which he hopes to mobilize against Britain. He plays with
the metaphor of 'the mother country' in a way that exposes
Britain as an unnatural parent. Having thereby implicitly
established norms for what it is to be a good parent, he
then appeals directly to his readers' own sense of their
responsibilities. 'As parents, we can have no joy, knowing
that this government [of England over America] is not
sufficiently lasting to insure any thing we may bequeath to
posterity . . . to discover the line of our duty rightly, we
should take our children in our hand, and fix our station a
few years further into life' (I. 21). As good parents we must
reject Britain's example and recognize the necessity of independence to make safe our children's future. Paine builds
his rhetorical appeal to a climax by demanding of his readers:

Hath your house been burnt? Hath your property been
destroyed before your face? Are your wife and children

41

destitute of a bed to lie upon or bread to live on? Have you
lost a parent or child by their hands, and yourself the
ruined and wretched survivor . . . if you have, and can
still shake hands with the murderers, then you are
unworthy the name husband, father, friend or lover. [I.
22–3]

As parents, lovers, and friends, Americans are duty-bound
to resist the tyranny of Britain. Her use of force against
the colonies, because unnatural, has made reconciliation
impossible, for 'there are injuries which nature cannot
forgive; she would cease to be nature if she did. As well can
the lover forgive the ravisher of his mistress, as the continent forgive the murders of Britain' (I. 30). The examples
of murder, rape, and other intrusions of force and violence
into the relationships closest to men's hearts are designed
to elicit and legitimate powerful emotions in his readers:

The Almighty hath implanted in us these unextin-
guishable feelings for good and wise purposes. They
are the guardians of his image in our hearts. They
distinguish us from the herd of common animals. The
social contract would dissolve and justice be extirpated
from the earth, or have only a casual existence were we
callous to the touches of affection. The robber and the
murderer would often escape punishment, did not the
injuries which our tempers sustain provoke us to justice.
[I. 30]

A sense of natural justice and a right of retribution are thus
implanted in the human frame; they are crucial aspects of
the 'true character of a man', and form the basis of—and
legitimate—our common sense of right and wrong.

It is this common sense, which British aggression has
outraged, which now demands independence, and which
unites Americans in a shared conception of the public good.
The outbreak of hostilities against the colonies 'softened

the whole body of the people into a degree of pliability, which laid the principal foundation-stone of union, order, and government' (I. 86). As in the opening parable, necessity, 'like a gravitating power', has forged a common bond of affection and obligation and a shared conception of the common good which ensures that people freely recognize their duties to the community. The new republic is not just a machine for co-ordinating and satisfying individual interests; it is a community of sentiment and belief, a new moral order, in which all may live according to their true nature and character as free, equal, and just citizens.

Paine believes that nature and common sentiment encourage the identification of the individual with the public good. But he also believes that this identification must be brought to people's consciousness (and fixed in the political institutions of the republic). While necessity and adversity have a part to play, so too does Paine. He writes: 'On the part of the public, my intention is, to show them their true and solid interest; to encourage them to their own good, to remove the fears and falsities which bad men have spread, and weak men have encouraged; and to excite in all men a love for union, and a cheerfulness for duty' (I. 69). And again: 'My principal design is to form the disposition of the people to the measures which I am fully persuaded it is in their interest and duty to adopt, and which need no other force to accomplish them than the force of being felt' (I. 182).

He brings a wide range of rhetorical skills to his task. He captures inchoate sentiments, latches on to subliminal fears and desires, and flatters people's pride so as to render the path of disinterested virtue appealing. But the true measure of his abilities is that he succeeds not just with the wealthy élite which has always dominated the political life of the nation, but with an extremely wide audience drawn predominantly from the middling and artisan ranks of colonial society. Paine's inclusion of such people is fully intentional; it is these men (not women) who will form the major block of voters in elections to State assemblies and to Congress, and their support, financial, political, and practical, is indispensable in the struggle for independence. Therefore they must be won over. For, unless they identify their individual good with the public good, there can be no question of independence or republican government.

Commerce, wealth, and property

In classical republican theory, wealth and luxury are seen as a fatal threat to the identification of individual with public good. Inequality is a source of social divisions and class conflict, which inevitably lead to the domination of one class over all the others and to the subordination of all interests to those of the dominant class. The result is a tyranny, of either the rich (oligarchy) or the poor (anarchy). Without a substantial degree of material equality between citizens there can be no civic virtue and no republic. Against the classical tradition, with its insistence on an austere agrarian economy, English Country Party theorists argued that the preservation of liberty depends on the existence of a class of independent property-owners whose moderate wealth enables them to resist the corrupting influence of the court and its luxury, yet gives them sufficient stake in the country to encourage the identification of their individual interests with the public good. In this tradition, citizenship is restricted to freeholders, whose property in land makes them reliable and distinguishes them from *hoi polloi*, or the mob.

Against both traditions, Paine denies the need for agrarian laws, and advocates a wide democratic suffrage not based on property holdings. He does not believe that a free commercial society with democratic institutions will be torn apart by class conflict. Nor does he accept that only those with landed property should be admitted to full citizenship. In each case Paine's rejection of the traditional

arguments rests on his conviction that a democratic Constitution establishes an equality of rights and freedoms
(including security of property) for all citizens which is not
threatened by inequalities of wealth or by majority rule, and
which does not jeopardize the achievement of the public
good. In this society, commerce may thrive with all its
benefits, and with no apparent risks. His conviction rests on
the assumption that each citizen will place more value on the
rights and freedoms which government protects equally for
all than on any particular interest which may run against the
rights or freedoms of others. No true citizen will countenance infringing the equal liberties of others for gain. This is
partly a matter of prudence, for once the liberties of one
citizen are violated, those of every other citizen become less
sacrosanct (II. 372). It is also, as we shall see below, partly a
matter of justice and reason, for where justice and reason
reign, neither commerce and its resulting inequalities nor
the democratic representation of the common people can
threaten the stability of the republic. But it is also because
commerce itself plays an integrative role in society.

Commerce is a major civilizing and socializing force. By
making possible the exchange of commodities, it makes
possible the development of civilization. Instead of each
person in the state of nature competing with all others to
secure the necessities of life, commerce allows us to help
satisfy the needs and desires of others, while expanding the
horizons of our own needs and desires (II. 240–2). Goods are
exchanged at their value, and labour and talents receive
their just reward; therefore, there is no place for class conflict. Moreover, every citizen can see that his or her individual good is best advanced by the maintenance of the
system as a whole. To this extent, Paine endorses Montesquieu's suggestion that the virtues associated with
commerce—economy, moderation, labour, prudence, and
so on—are perfectly compatible with civic virtue and public
spirit. This is not to say that commerce necessarily

45

encourages virtue. Indeed, England provides a case in point; for 'with the increase in commerce England hath lost its spirit . . . The more men have to lose, the less they are willing to venture. The rich are in general slaves to fear, and submit to courtly power with the trembling duplicity of a spaniel' (I. 36). Nevertheless Paine believes that this relationship between commerce and the decline of virtue in England was contingent, not necessary. Although his comments are sparse, he seems to believe that in monarchies commerce is inimical to liberty and public spirit, because court wealth and patronage exaggerate economic and social divisions and destroy the natural, just, reasonable connection between the abilities, talents, and efforts of citizens and the rewards they receive. In a republic men may earn the respect of their fellow citizens through their talents and virtues, and may rise to positions of social influence and political power as a result, thereby serving both their own good and that of the public. In a monarchy no such connection exists, since influence and power belong to a hereditary class of sycophants, idlers, and wasters. It is small wonder that commerce has little positive effect in such a context; for where the public realm does not respect men of talent and ability, such men will not respect the public realm. They will turn instead to their own interests and grow rich and soft, corruptible and malleable.

This fate awaits America if she remains dependent on Britain; her youthful virtue will be lost, and she will sink into luxury and decadence. But if she marshals her virtue and builds a republic, the world will see a remarkable transformation. The republic-in-arms will be succeeded by a meritocratic civic culture dominated by industry and commerce, in which government activity is limited and the citizens' virtue is subject to fewer demands. The world has seen America in adversity, 'rising in resolution as the storm increased' (I. 231). America must now show that 'she can bear prosperity; and that her honest virtue in time of peace, is equal to her bravest virtue in time of war'. She must descend to 'the scenes of quiet and domestic life . . . to enjoy her own land, and under her own vine, the sweet of her labours and the reward of her toil' (I. 231). The post-revolutionary republic is a remarkably sedate—a very civil—society (II. 293).

There is no fear that the citizenry will become corrupted by wealth and disrupted by faction and class conflict. Paine's portrait of the new America is of a society regulated by the concurrence and co-ordinated satisfaction of people's desires and needs—that is, by commerce—rather than by the activities of government, a society flourishing under a Constitution which, by granting political equality and liberty to each individual, will preserve the glowing coal of freedom. The citizens of such a society will not need a stake in landed property to feel committed to the public good and to be willing to spring to its defence in time of need, because all will share equally in a 'property' for which they are prepared to make the greatest sacrifices: 'Property alone cannot defend a country against invading enemies . . . the defence must be personal, and that which equally unites all must be something equally the property of all, viz., an equal share of freedom, independent of varieties of wealth' (II. 288). The individual finds his or her good in the public good, because the public good involves protection of the freedom and rights of each and a guarantee of fundamental political equality for all. Where the older republicanism stressed the material conditions necessary for the prevention of class conflict and the development of citizen virtue, Paine regards these as relatively insignificant when placed against the equality of freedom and rights which the republic assures its citizens. Nevertheless, his lack of concern about the long-term effects of commerce on the nation reveals a more basic departure from the republican tradition.

Classical republicanism sought to harness man's fallen nature by means of a range of institutional mechanisms which would bring about a conjunction between individual

47

Paine

passions and interests and the common good. Republics were seen as delicate feats of social engineering which required certain demographic, economic, social, cultural, and sometimes geographical and climatic conditions for their survival. Reason and rationality played little part in the tradition—indeed, it is precisely because of the frailty of human reason that this feat of social engineering was deemed necessary. Against this tradition, Paine emphasizes the unity generated by the equality of rights and freedoms. He believes that citizens in the new republic will support the public good because they will recognize that it embodies rational principles of justice and liberty.

The force of reason

Paine's belief that reason and rationality will effect the reconciliation of the individual and the public good developed slowly. In *Common Sense* and his *Crisis* letters, his emphasis upon government shaping 'the general manners and morality of a country' (I. 117) echoes the concerns of classical republicanism; moreover, he saw a positive role for government in 'the encouragement and protection of the good subjects of any state, and the suppression and punishment of bad ones' (I. 97). This and other comments (cf. II. 63) suggest that the identification of the good of the individual with the public good might legitimately be brought about by coercion. However, his later writings, particularly after the Revolution, place a much greater emphasis on reason. The inherent virtues of republican government will eventually establish themselves because 'that which is right will become popular, and that which is wrong, though by mistake it may obtain the cry or fashion of the day, will soon lose the power of delusion, and sink into disesteem' (I. 197). Once the people understand the value of free government, the news will spread with truly revolutionary repercussions:

Kings will go out of fashion in the same way as conjurers did. . . . the decline of superstition, the great increase and diffusion of knowledge, and the frequent equalities of merit in individuals, would render it impossible to decorate any one man with the idolatrous honours which are expected to be paid to him under the name of crowned head. [II. 290]

Once the virtues of a republic are known, people will not settle for less; for 'The mind once enlightened cannot again become dark. . . . There is no possibility, neither is there any term to express the supposition by; of the mind *un*knowing anything it already knows' (II. 244). The reason why individuals will support the public good and republican government and will not fall into luxury, corruption, and faction as commerce increases their wealth and creates certain material inequalities is that they will recognize the rightness and reasonableness of the thing. By the time he wrote his *Letter to the Abbé Raynal* in 1782, he was prepared to argue that history has shown a progressive path from barbarism to civilization, and that the future holds the prospect of civilizing relations between nations. Just as commerce once formed men into societies to furnish their wants and harmonize their interests, so it will now do the same between nations, aided by the progress of reason and enlightenment (II. 241–2).

Throughout Paine's writings on independence and the Revolution runs tension between his subscription to aspects of republicanism and his subscription to facets of natural-rights theories (although the tension is hardly exclusive to Paine). But although Paine occasionally seems willing to sacrifice individual rights to the public good, for the most part he believes that it is possible to combine the two traditions so as to give full protection for rights while at the same time sustaining a substantive conception of the common good. We have considered three possible grounds for his belief that the two traditions are not in conflict: his appeal to the common sentiments and feelings of a community, his argument that commerce integrates a community by co-ordinating the satisfaction of people's needs, and his direct appeal to rationality and the progress of reason. This last, later development brings out the rationalist underpinning which his earlier appeals to feelings and sentiment and common interests only implied. It also allows Paine to go a long way towards resolving the tension in his ideas. All he need do is argue that natural rights belong to all human beings *qua* rational creatures and that they are protected and supported only in so far as their bearers continue to act as rational human beings, which in turn involves recognizing, when reason demands, that they lend their support to the public good.

To the modern reader this position sounds either coercive or naïve—coercive, because it seems to allow natural rights to be swept aside by the imperious demands of the public good, simply by labelling those who resist as irrational; naïve, if Paine really believes that people will recognize in the public good the demands of reason and justice. But, serious as these allegations are, neither is really justified. Paine's commitment to the natural and civil rights of citizens is real enough, and after the Revolution it was further demonstrated by his growing recognition that majority rule could involve serious infringements of individual rights and his unequivocal denunciation of any such infringement in his *Dissertations on Government* (1786). He writes that, when a people form a republic, 'they renounce, as detestable, the power of exercising, at any future time any species of despotism over each other, or doing a thing not right in itself, because a majority of them have the strength of numbers sufficient to accomplish it' (II. 373). This recognition of the despotic potential of democratic rule may be belated, but it is none the less sincere, as is his defence of individual rights in his later works.

The allegation of naïvety is less easily dismissed. Whether someone's judgements are naïve does not depend solely on the content of their beliefs. Their judgements must be assessed not according to general, eternal criteria of critical rationality (since such criteria are hardly close to hand), but with regard to the intellectual and practical context in which the beliefs in question were formed. Paine was hardly a seasoned pamphleteer when he wrote *Common Sense*. He had only one previous, unpublished pamphlet and a number of newspaper articles to his credit. Although he tended to exaggerate his lack of experience, as if to imply that the cause of America was his sole inspiration and motive, the lack was real enough. *Common Sense* fused the legacy of his involvement in political debate and discussion during his time in England with the traditions of radical republicanism with which he first came into contact through friends and acquaintances in Philadelphia. The result is a heady, but not entirely satisfactory, product. Many of his comments smack of presumption, bravado, and wishful thinking; and there are many fine turns of phrase, 'manly' sentiments, and passionate denunciations and declarations. This is radical rhetoric unsullied by the grim realities which were to follow. In retrospect it reveals a predominance of style over substance. This is not to deny the probably considerable—but certainly unmeasurable—impact of this rhetoric on his audience. It is simply to insist that the buoyant optimism must have seemed breathtakingly naïve, not least to Paine, in the years that followed. The latter were hard times, 'the times that try men's souls', (I. 50), and they brought forth a grittier rhetoric, one able to capture and bolster the now less confident imaginations of men and women who had seen the more brutal and daunting face of the struggle for independence. The arguments are now more detailed, more pragmatic, and more urgent; Paine's narrative skills are frequently called on as the pamphlets come to double as propaganda and newspapers; the appeals to Providence now rely more on the hope and faith of the reader than on his or her powers of induction; and the choice for America becomes increasingly stark—freedom or subjection, slavery, and plunder. The heights of Paine's republican rhetoric, the appeals to the common good, civic virtues, and duties to cause, country, and children are reached in the *Crisis* letters, particularly those written at the most desperate times for the continental forces. After the fall of Yorktown and the recognition of both sides that independence had been secured, Paine looked back over events with the benefit of hindsight, and found in the triumph of the American cause the triumph of right over might, reason over superstition, and liberty over despotism. He now saw Providence as the force of reason breaking apart the fetters of ignorance in the cause of liberty and free government—the march of reason through history! America is no longer the last bastion in the defence of liberty; it is the founder of the new, enlightened universal order: 'The true idea of a great nation, is that which extends and promotes universal society; whose mind rises above the atmosphere of local thoughts, and considers mankind, of whatever nation or profession they may be, as the work of one Creator' (II. 256).

Nothing succeeds like success, and little else is as persuasive. Paine's revolutionary experiences and the successful outcome of the struggle led him to develop and substantiate principles and beliefs which he had only hinted at earlier.

His increasing willingness to appeal to reason is evidence of his own realization that what had once seemed a matter only of necessity and interest was in fact of more universal significance. This conviction never left Paine, and has seldom left America. It marked all his subsequent political theory, but it is difficult to dismiss it as naïve. Historians have found more intellectually compelling and prosaic explanations for the American Revolution and its success, but those who lived through the events and saw them in terms of the political theories and eschatology of the day could hardly be expected to have searched rigorously for the causal conditions of their beliefs. The rightness of the cause and the triumph of right and reason over the darker forces of despotism must have struck many besides Paine as a perfectly adequate explanation for the course of events, and hence sufficient to ground the expectations of the new age.

3 Europe

The Rights of Man: Part One

> In the first part of "*Rights of Man*" I have endeavoured
> to show . . . that there does not exist a right to establish
> hereditary government . . . because hereditary govern-
> ment always means a government yet to come, and the
> case always is, that the people who are to live afterwards,
> have always the same right to choose a government for
> themselves, as the people had who have lived before
> them. [II. 447]

Paine had attacked 'the hereditary system' in *Common
Sense*. He had argued that, 'all men being originally equal,
no one by birth could have a right to set up his own family
in perpetual preference to all others for ever'; that nature
clearly disapproves of such a system, 'otherwise she could
not so frequently turn it to ridicule, by giving mankind an
ass for a lion'; and that while men may consent to another's
rule, they cannot 'without manifest injustice to their
children say "that your children and your children's
children shall reign over ours forever", because such an
unwise, unjust, unnatural compact might (perhaps) in the
next succession put them under the government of a rogue
or a fool' (I. 13). In *Common Sense* Paine did not discuss
these points at length; but in the first part of his *Rights of
Man* he elaborates and extends his claims, and makes a
detailed, cogent attack on the hereditary system. In doing
so, he also distinguishes between natural and civil rights,
and develops a range of arguments on the related issues of
constitutions, popular sovereignty, universal suffrage, and
representative government. There are foretastes of all these
arguments in Paine's American writings, but it was the

French Revolution and Burke's virulent defence of the status quo which gave him the opportunity to transform his until then rather loosely formulated position into a fully-fledged natural-rights justification of representative government and the ultimate sovereignty of the people. At the same time, using a range of literary and rhetorical devices, he turned these theoretical principles into a blistering attack on Burke's *Reflections* and its attempt to justify the social and political inequalities of Britain.

The principles

Paine introduced his theory of rights in the course of challenging Burke's account of the principles of 1688. In his *Discourse on the Love of our Country* (1788), a commemorative address on the centennial of the Glorious Revolution, Richard Price had argued that in the Revolution the people had legitimately exercised their rights to choose their governors, to cashier them for misconduct, and to frame a government for themselves. Taking Price's address as the initial focus for his attack on the principles of the French Revolution, Burke denied that any such rights inhered in a nation and that the Glorious Revolution proved their existence. He cited a parliamentary statute of the time which claimed 'to bind us [the people of the day], our *heirs* and our *posterity*, to *them* [William and Mary], their *heirs*, and *posterity*, to the end of time'; and went on to say: 'So far is it from being true, that we acquired a right by the Revolution to elect our kings, that if we had possessed it before, the English Nation did at that time most solemnly renounce and abdicate it, for themselves and for all their posterity for ever' (EB 104).

Against Burke, Paine insists that 'there never can be a parliament, or any description of men, or any generation of men, in any country, possessed of the right or the power of binding and controlling posterity to "the end of time".' On the contrary, 'every age and generation must be as free to act for itself *in all cases*, as the ages and generation which preceded it' (I. 251). Paine argues that if any group of people has a right to form a government and establish a set of powers to regulate its proceedings, and if it has this right simply by virtue of being human, then all groups must have this right. It is absurd to claim that what one group of people has a right to do *qua* human beings, subsequent generations have no right to do. Burke can only claim that those involved in the Revolution Settlement had a right which subsequent generations do not have if the right in question was a special rather than a natural right—that is, if it was a right awarded them by virtue of some feature common to them but lacking in subsequent generations. But what was this feature? Who had the right to confer such a special right? And where does the right to confer special rights come from? As Paine shows, the problem with arguments from historical precedent is that they do not go back far enough. To base claims about rights on precedent, we must go back all the way; but then 'we shall come to the time when man came from the hand of his Maker'. The divine creation is the divine origin of the rights of man: there can be no higher authority. But this authority simply confirms what Paine calls the 'unity of man', the principle that we are all born equal in the sight of God and therefore have equal natural rights. It follows that no man can claim to be divinely chosen to rule, and that the rights of one generation must be the same as the rights of every other generation. If one generation has the right to submit to a hereditary monarch, then all generations must have this right; but if all generations have this right, then no generation has it.

Burke's claims are not so easily dismissed, however. Paine's position relies on an interpretation of natural rights which Burke sees as wildly abstract and metaphysical. Burke has no wish to deny that there are certain natural rights—that is, rights which must be recognized as belonging to individuals in a natural state. While his account of these rights is sketchy, he notes that the right to self-preservation is a basic law of nature, as is the right of each to govern himself (EB 150–1). The content of these rights is not all that important, however, since in becoming a member of civil society, each individual must surrender or transfer these rights in exchange for the advantages which membership brings. It is these advantages which Burke refers to as the 'real rights of men'. Civil society is an 'institution of beneficence', and law is 'beneficence acting by a rule. Men have a right to live by that rule, they have a right to justice . . . they have a right to the fruits of their industry . . . they have a right to the acquisitions of their parents; to the nourishment and improvement of their off-spring; to instruction in life, and to consolation in death' (EB 149). The rights or advantages of civil society can be secured only if each individual surrenders 'the first fundamental right of uncovenanted man, that is the right to judge for himself, and to assert his own cause'. For 'Man cannot enjoy the rights of an uncivil and of a civil state together' (EB 150): in the former, men's passions are unconstrained; in the latter, 'the inclinations of men should frequently be thwarted, their will controlled, and their passions brought into subjection' (EB 151). To secure the advantages of civil society, men must submit to rule '*by a power out of themselves*' (Burke's emphasis), which cannot be 'subject to that will and those passions which it is its office to bridle and subdue'. That is, in surrendering the right to self-government, men forfeit any claim to participation in the government and politics of their society. 'The whole organisation of government becomes a consideration of convenience'; and the rights which men have in the state of nature are of no relevance to the issue of convenience. If hereditary government can be shown to be convenient, the fact that it denies political rights to the vast majority of its subjects cannot be claimed to undermine its legitimacy.

Paine

Burke's view of society provides unequivocal support for the hereditary system. Society is a dense fabric of institutions, laws, rules, norms, values, and meanings, which can be sustained only if it commands the respect of its members, and if they recognize their obligation to their ancestors and their posterity to preserve it intact. A contract underlies society, but it is not the kind of contract used in commerce 'or some other such low concern'. It is better understood as a partnership 'between those who are living, those who are dead, and those who are to be born'. The goals of the partnership are given by a higher order of nature:

> Each contract of each particular state is but a clause in the great primaeval contract of eternal society, linking the lower with the higher natures, connecting the visible and invisible world, according to a fixed compact sanctioned by the inviolable oath which holds all physical and moral natures, each in their appointed place. [EB 195]

The hierarchical order is convenient because natural, and natural because divinely ordered.

There is little place for fundamental reform in this order. By the 'unprincipled facility of changing the state as often, and as much, and in as many ways as there are floating fancies or fashions, the whole chain and continuity of the commonwealth would be broken' (EB 193). Radical change cannot be a just or reasonable objective of intentional choice:

> . . . if that which is only submission to necessity should be made the object of choice, the law is broken, nature is disobeyed, and the rebellious are outlawed, cast forth, and exiled, from this world of reason, and order, and peace, and virtue, and fruitful penitence, into the antagonistic world of madness, discord, vice, confusion and unavailing sorrow. [EB 195]

The subject's duty is to submit to this order of 'fruitful

penitence'; there can be no question of conceding the majority political rights which would allow them to subvert it.

Given this analysis, the question of hereditary right becomes much more complex. For Burke the issue is not one of hereditary right versus representative government, but of hereditary right versus the anarchy of the natural state. Surrender of the rights of anarchy for the privileges of the social order is so reasonable an exchange that it makes no sense to claim that people's rights are infringed by the creation of a hereditary monarchy and its attendant system of rule. In Burke's view, to insist that one generation cannot bind its successors is to throw each generation into a state in which their rights are equal to their passions, in which order is destroyed, and in which each is stripped of the benefits of society, leaving (in King Lear's words) 'unaccommodated man—a poor, bare, forked animal'.

Paine's initial case against hereditary right seems less compelling in the light of this more complex argument. Yet it is unclear quite how one might proceed to refute Burke's claims. Some commentators have maintained that Paine never really engages Burke's argument, but relies instead on a series of contrary assertions which merely repeat his old views. This is to overstate the case, however; for it is in the *Rights of Man* that Paine first grounds his political theory wholly on a theory of natural rights and popular sovereignty. Moreover, these innovations are the fruit of his labours on the *Reflections*, and it is in the detail of this theory that Paine's refutation of Burke is fully expounded.

In direct contrast to Burke, Paine argues that men's natural rights are not surrendered upon entering civil society. On the contrary, civil rights are rooted in natural rights; for 'Man did not enter into society to become worse than he was before, nor to have fewer rights than he had before, but to have those rights better secured. His natural rights are the foundation of all his civil rights' (I. 275). He argues that we have two kinds of natural rights: those which we naturally have the power to execute, as in the case of the right to conscience; and those which we lack the natural power to exercise, as in the case of rights to security and protection from violation and the right to redress. We always have the right and the power to *judge* when someone has treated us unjustly, but we do not always have the power to enforce our right to redress. Where the power to execute a right is defective, the individual 'depositeth his right in the common stock of society, and takes the arm of society, of which he is a part, in preference and in addition to his own' (I. 276). Society gives us nothing: we have a natural right to redress, and when we call on society for aid, we draw on a common stock to which we have contributed. Moreover, society can have no jurisdiction over those rights with regard to which the power to execute is perfect—for example, the right to religious belief. In its essentials this account is similar to that of Locke, who also saw the function of society in terms of more perfectly securing our natural rights. Although Paine's case is less sharply formulated than Locke's, its basic claim is unmistakable. Civil rights remain rooted in natural rights; together, the two kinds provide the indefeasible framework within which legitimate civil authorities must operate. This is why he includes both natural and civil rights when discussing declarations of the rights of man. The social compact must guarantee protection for both types of natural rights. 'The aim of men gathered together in society being the maintenance of their natural, civil and political rights, these rights are the basis of the social compact, and their recognition and their declaration should precede the constitution which assures their guarantee' (II. 558).

The social compact is indeed 'social' in nature: it forms a *society* to act as the guardian, not the giver, of the individual's rights (II. 584). By collecting the power of each individual, the compact creates a nation in which the people as a whole are sovereign. Each person remains individually sovereign in those areas in which right and power are equivalent; but each accepts the sovereign power of the nation as guarantor of his or her imperfect natural rights when they are unequal.

Burke's contract is a contract of submission to a ruler; whereas the contract of Locke and Paine is a contract of association among equals for their mutual protection and benefit, a contract which establishes a society in which the people as a whole are sovereign. This sovereign people then draws up a Constitution which provides the framework and the principles of government, and government then acts as a trustee of this sovereignty. This means that constitutions, governments, laws, and executive acts are not, and cannot be, binding on the ultimate sovereignty of the people.

Although Paine does not spell it out, in deference to the Constitution of 1789 which he was defending, an implicit corollary of his argument (as becomes clear in his later work) is that true popular sovereignty requires universal suffrage—defective natural rights are exchanged for the right to participate in national sovereignty. National, popular sovereignty secures all natural rights equally by substituting the collective will and power for the will and power of individuals where their power is unequal to their rights. Right and power become equal and thus perfect (principally in matters of protection and security) through the sovereignty of the nation; and just as individual perfect natural rights are inalienable, so too is the perfect right of the sovereign people.

The nation's right to self-government is derived from its constituent individuals' rights to self-government and self-development. This right finds its expression in the popular will, manifested in either elections or public opinion, and is matched by an equivalent power. The people may cede certain powers to a form of public authority, but they retain the right to judge how well this trust is executed, and necessarily have the power collectively to enforce that

61

judgement. When Paine argues that the people are sovereign, he is simply saying that government rests ultimately on opinion. A nation has a perfect natural right to will what it wills, and it cannot be bound to will something—for example, a form of government—which in fact it no longer wills. A nation may mistake its true interests, and may confer absolute power on an individual whom it styles 'king'; but should it cease to believe that its interests are best served in this way, the king has no claim against it and is rendered powerless. 'For a nation to be free it is sufficient that she wills it' (I. 322, II. 496, and elsewhere).

Constitutions and the governments to which they give rise are expressions of this sovereign will. But if they cease to express the 'common sense' of the nation, they have no legitimacy. They may manipulate opinion by means of fraud and superstition, or they may attempt to rule by coercion. But without popular sanction, they cannot survive long. This does not mean that a Constitution must have the unanimous support of the people. Each member has the right to give an opinion, but no one has the right to demand that his or her opinion govern the rest. The social compact guarantees each person a say in the collective affairs of the nation, but the will of the nation necessarily rests with the majority voice. Nevertheless, national sovereignty cannot justly transgress the natural and civil rights of the people, because its sole *raison d'être* is the defence of these rights. This is clear from Paine's earlier comments in *Dissertations on Government* (1786). National sovereignty is not an unlimited sovereignty of the popular will; its scope is delimited by the purpose for which it is brought into existence—namely, to defend its members' equal natural rights.

The sovereign in a republic is exercised to keep right and wrong in their proper and distinct places, and never suffer the one to usurp the place of the other. A republic, properly understood, is a sovereignty of justice, in contradistinction to a sovereignty of will. [II. 375]

Although national sovereignty cannot be alienated (for example, given over in perpetuity to a king and his heirs), it can be suppressed, as when a people is ruled by force and fraud (the characteristic supports of the hereditary system). None the less, the right and the power remain with the people; all they need is the will to exercise them. 'A nation has at all times an inherent indefeasible right to abolish any form of government it finds inconvenient, and establish such as accords with its interest, disposition and happiness' (I. 341). Britain retains its monarchy not because it does not have the right to discard it (on the contrary), but because the people have not yet come to see their interest clearly. The *Rights of Man* leaves no room for doubt as to why the people have failed to perceive the imposture: the hereditary system overawes people with ritual and splendour, intimidates them with shows of force and threats of eternal damnation, and bewilders them with its sophistical claims about their eternal duties to the Crown, the nobility, the Church, and the State. Paine denounces Burke's pamphlet as part of this system of fraud and imposture, and offers the *Rights of Man* as an antidote which, by exposing these frauds, will provide the nation with the opportunity to will freedom for itself.

This more complex argument against Burke shows that the long-standing practices, traditions, past agreements, and prescriptive rights which Burke emphasizes must be weighed on the scales of current public opinion. Their legitimacy is a function not of their longevity, but of the weight they are accorded by this opinion. Indeed, Paine sees that Burke himself recognizes this, and that the *Reflections* are a carefully contrived attempt to bolster support for the existing conventions and practices of government among an élite whose dominance depends on the quiescence and deference of the majority of the population, those whom 'providence dooms to live on trust' (EB 195). Similarly, the *Rights of Man* is not just an argument for the principle of popular sovereignty; it is also a direct appeal to the sovereign public. By exposing the frauds which Burke seeks to perpetrate and perpetuate; by appealing to reason and evidence as the only valid criteria for belief, as against Burke's conjuring with the emotions, prejudices, habits, and customs of his audience; and by directing his arguments to the very people whose 'tacit consent' or acquiescence underpins the existing system of rule, Paine seeks to destroy the fabric of opinion which supports the hereditary system. The legitimacy of the existing order stands or falls precisely according to the prevailing opinion of the people, and it is to this court of appeal that Paine submits his work.

The force of the argument

The force of Paine's appeal to the people rests as much on the way he presents his message as on its content. The *Rights of Man* is a carefully planned and executed piece of rhetoric, designed to galvanize the artisan and middling classes in support of reform and the French cause. That said, it must be admitted that it does not look much like a classic text of modern political thought, and it is not surprising, therefore, to find a sympathetic reviewer describing its style as 'desultory, uncouth, and inelegant (*Monthly Review* V (1791), p. 81).' If we are to understand the impact of the pamphlet on Paine's contemporaries, however, we must recognize that, far from detracting from its force, the pamphlet's disorganized appearance is a central plank of Paine's strategy against Burke.

Paine believes that hereditary systems rely on a mixture of political imposture, force, and the ignorance of the mass of the people. He sees Burke's *Reflections* as an appeal to the élite to maintain the imposture, and he writes Part One to expose this fraud to the middling and lower orders of society, and thereby undermine the legitimacy of the existing political order. Both his prose style, which is forceful and direct and his 'desultory' presentation are intended to facilitate communication with people who have little education and little experience of political debate. He makes his points briskly, frequently using a pair of pithy sentences to catch the reader's attention and express the main thrust of the argument, and following this with a longer sentence elaborating the message.

> Every generation is, and must be, competent to all the purposes which its occasions require. It is the living, and not the dead, that are to be accommodated. When man ceases to be, his power and his wants cease with him; and having no longer any participation in the concerns of this world, he has no longer any authority in directing who shall be its governors, or how its government shall be organised, or how administered. [I. 251]

He repeats his points two or three times on a page, and returns to them again and again throughout the pamphlet. He presents his argument in short bursts, and does not try to build long chains of deductive reasoning. He switches cleanly from one topic to the next, without long preambles or introductory remarks, and thus avoids overwhelming his audience and succeeds in holding its interest. By this means, he comes across to the reader as scoring success after success in his attack. In expressing himself in blunt, unmannered, transparent prose, he presents himself as a simple, unpretentious man of common intelligence and some experience of the world who seeks to bring Burke's ideas to the court of common sense. This authorial persona stands him in good stead in dealing with Burke's more metaphysical notions:

> But, after all, what is this metaphor called a crown, or rather what is a monarchy? Is it a thing, or is it a name, or is it a fraud? Is it a 'contrivance of human wisdom,' or human craft, to obtain money from a nation under specious pretences? Is it a thing necessary to a nation? If it is, in what does this necessity consist, what service does it perform, what is its business, and what are its merits? Does the virtue consist in the metaphor, or in the man? Doth the goldsmith that makes the crown, make the virtue also? [I. 325]

It also enables him to present himself as an impartial spectator of the events of the Revolution, as against Burke, whose account is nothing more 'than a tale accommodated to his own passions and prejudices . . . a set of paintings by which Mr Burke has outraged his own imagination!'

Further, Paine uses Burke's arguments to offend his readers' sensibilities. Whereas Paine contemplates 'the natural dignity of man' and the honour and happiness of his character, he portrays Burke as regarding man as caught up with 'foppery', 'childishness', and a fascination with 'baubles' and 'gewgaws', and as lacking the sense and reason to judge for himself how society should conduct its collective affairs (I. 286–7). If Paine's readers are going to accept Burke's arguments, they must also accept that they are poor, barely rational beings. By contrast, Paine extends to them citizenship in a republic of political discussion and a right of appeal against injustice in the court of reason. Above all, he addresses his readers as equals. He sets before them arguments which he has found convincing, and conveys to them a sense that they are reasonable people who are well able to see through the imposture of the hereditary system and assert their natural rights. By writing in a manner immediately accessible to men and women with little formal education who had until then been regarded as too vulgar to participate in the refined and civilized art of political discourse, he was able to bring them to see themselves, for the first time, as having the capacity and the right to enter political debate. In so doing, Paine puts into question—in the sense of both making debatable and making uncertain—the legitimacy of the prevailing political order.

The invitation to citizenship

Having sought to turn his audience of subjects into citizens in Part One of the *Rights of Man*, he attempts to turn them into revolutionaries in Part Two. Now that he has 'the ear of John Bull' (II. 1322), he drives home both the reasonableness of the republican system of government and its eminent practicability, and does so against the backdrop of the people's indefeasible right to judge. His success in conveying this message can be judged by the massive sales of the *Rights of Man*—conservative estimates put the figure at more than 100,000 copies sold by 1793—and by the determination with which the Government sought to prevent its distribution.

The refutation of Burke's *Reflections* has been called a 'one-finger exercise in politics and history' (RW 24). This is nonsense. It badly underestimates Burke, and fails to give due recognition to the hard theoretical work which Paine puts into his *Rights of Man*. It implies that the 'debate on France' was simply a further rehearsal of well-worn arguments for and against the rights of man and political reform. Yet the debate was important precisely because it was only through the process of argument and counter-argument it entailed that many of the principles of both radicals and conservatives were developed. Although Paine describes himself in Part One as setting out to show that there did not exist a right of hereditary succession, we mistake his project and the nature of political struggles if we see him as concerned only with providing a consistent set of alternative principles. He also hoped to destroy the credibility of both Burke's case and the system which it supported. This was no one-finger exercise; it required all Paine's considerable skills as a polemicist, journalist, and political theorist to produce a text which could begin to fray the fabric of opinion upon which the British government relied for its legitimacy. In the process and under the influence of both the French proclamation of natural rights and Burke's repudiation of them as 'paltry scraps of paper', he developed for the first time the outlines of a natural rights-based theory of popular sovereignty and democratic government freed from the republican tenets and tensions which we noted in his American writings. It is this outline which is developed in Part Two into a fully-fledged account of the principles, institutions, and ends of representative government.

Rights of Man: Part Two

It is in Part Two of his *Rights of Man* and his subsequent writings on France that Paine makes some of his most original contributions to political theory. Like *Common Sense*, Part Two begins by distinguishing between society and government; but if the distinction is the same, the conclusions he draws are substantially different. Whereas in *Common Sense* the ideal state lies in the past, in a society without government, united by necessity and uncorrupted by vice; in Paine's later writings, the ideal state lies in the future, and the past is seen as a period of barbarism which is giving way only gradually to the development of 'universal civilisation'. Universal civilization involves the full flourishing of society, which increasingly obviates the need for government. Moreover, Paine's case for the progressive nature of social change rests not on a utopian optimism, but on a relatively sophisticated account of the relationship between economic, social, and political development. Paine sees people as naturally sociable and as bound together by mutual interest and

reciprocal dependence. 'Common interest regulates their
concerns, and forms their laws; and the laws which
common usage ordains, have a greater influence than
the laws of government. (I. 357)' This sociability and
interdependence are natural, because it is nature that has
made people's wants greater than their powers:

> No man is capable, without the aid of society, of supply-
> ing his own wants; and those wants acting upon every
> individual, impel the whole of them into society, as
> naturally as gravitation acts to a centre. But she [nature]
> has gone further. She has not only forced man into
> society, by a diversity of wants, which the reciprocal aid
> of each other can supply, but she has implanted in him
> a system of social affections, which, though not
> necessary to his existence, are essential to his happiness.
> There is no period of life when this love of society ceases
> to act. [I. 357]

Government is hardly required at all. Indeed, 'man is so
naturally a creature of society, that it is almost impossible
to put him out of it' (I. 358). The security and prosperity of
a people depend less on government than on the 'unceasing
circulation of interest, which passing through its million
channels, invigorates the whole mass of civilised man'; and
as society develops, government becomes increasingly
redundant:

> The more perfect civilisation is, the less occasion it has
> for government, because the more does it regulate its own
> affairs and govern itself. . . . All the great laws of society
> are laws of nature. Those of trade and commerce,
> whether with respect to the intercourse of individuals, or
> of nations, are laws of mutual and reciprocal interest.
> They are followed and obeyed because it is in the interest
> of the parties so to do. [I. 358–9]

Society is thus practically autonomous and self-regulating, the operation of interests, compounded by reason and social affections, sufficing to produce a stable social order. Commerce is the most perfect expression of such an order, for it unites mankind 'by rendering nations, as well as individuals, useful to each other' (I. 400). Moreover, it is sanctioned by Providence:

> . . . by the same rule that nature intended the intercourse of two [individuals], she intended that of all. For this purpose she has distributed the material of manufacturers and commerce in various distinct parts of a nation and of the world; and as they cannot be procured by war as cheaply or so commodiously as by commerce, she has rendered the latter the means of extirpating the former. [I. 400]

This new theme of the evolution of society from barbarism to 'universal civilisation' through the development of commerce, first mooted in Paine's *Letter to the Abbé Raynal* of 1782, lends substantial support to his new claims that the nations of Europe are ripe for revolution.

Paine sees the state as beginning with a body of armed men—or, more colourfully, a 'banditti of ruffians'—who use their superior force to exact tribute from the shepherds and herdsmen who graze the land. Once established, this body tries to convert might into right; thus 'the chief of the band contrive[s] to lose the name of robber in that of monarch' (I. 361). The expropriated wealth of the people finances the luxury of the court, by which the king corrupts those who might threaten his position and funds his imperial ambitions. Plunder is disguised as the legitimate obtaining of revenue, and the monopoly of violence is masked by the claim to hereditary right. The system remains destitute of principle and committed to a 'continual system of war and extortion', since monarchies are engaged in a continual struggle for power, prestige, and revenue, and war is their common instrument of policy (I. 399). Yet, almost miraculously and certainly providentially, despite such 'a long accumulating load of discouragement and oppression', the peaceful arts of agriculture, manufacture, and commerce have made gradual progress, thereby demonstrating that 'instinct in animals does not act with stronger impulse, than the principles of society and civilisation operate in man' (I. 363). As these peaceful arts develop, the tensions between society and hereditary government, between the interests of the people and those of the court, become increasingly stark, and the imposture of hereditary government becomes increasingly obvious. Moreover, Paine leaves us in no doubt as to how obvious it has become:

> It [hereditary government] is a system of mental levelling. It indiscriminately admits every species of character to the same authority. Vice and virtue, ignorance and wisdom, in short, every quality, good or bad, is put on the same level. Kings succeed each other, not as rationals, but as animals. . . . when we see that nature acts as if she disowned and sported with the hereditary system; that the mental characters of successors, in all countries, are below the average of human understanding; that one is a tyrant, another an idiot, a third insane, and some all three together, it is impossible to attach confidence to it. . . . It requires some talents to be a common mechanic; but to be a king, requires only the animal figure of a man—a sort of breathing automaton. [I. 365–6]

Kings are not naturally evil; it is their position in society which encourages all the vices and conceits of monarchy. Brought up to see themselves as superior, their capacity for sympathy with others never develops. 'What renders us kind and humane? Is it not sympathy, the power I have of putting myself in my neighbour's place? How can a monarch have sympathy?' Unsurprisingly, Paine's own sympathies for monarchs—which are considerable, given the standards of his fellow participants in the debates over the trial and execution of Louis XVI—are strictly limited. The common man's resentment of his subjection still burns within him: 'All that the noble asks of me is that I recognise his superiority because of his birth, while the king requires my submission: I am amused by the noble; I feel like setting my foot upon the king' (II. 545).

These are the sentiments of the new man, a man freed from dependence on a master and at liberty to pursue his interests and exercise his talents in the market, a man who weighs things at their value, recognizes only equals, and whose judgement is his own to exercise as he sees fit. When society has such people for citizens, the days of kings are numbered. Although Paine never fully elaborates a causal theory relating the division of labour and the consequent spread of commerce to the development of an educated, independent citizenry capable of penetrating the hereditary fraud and replacing it with representative government, such a theory is implicit throughout his later work. He is not so naïve as to see the American and French revolutions as the outcome solely of the spread of opinion. Although the obvious reasonableness of the representative system plays a crucial role in its acceptance, we underestimate Paine's sophistication as a political theorist if we fail to recognize that he is fully aware that deeper social and economic changes have prepared the way for the drawing of the new age.

Representative democracy

It is in the *Rights of Man* and his subsequent writings on France that Paine first develops the arguments for representative government founded on universal suffrage. But because representative government is so much a part of modern life in the West, we are liable to miss the fact that Paine's argument remains framed by the older republican paradigm which marked his writing on America. Paine formulates the political problem in terms of the following question: Under what system of government is power most likely to be exercised so as to promote the liberty, security, and well-being of all its citizens? Monarchy and aristocracy stand condemned because they rule by force and fraud in the interests of an individual or class and are necessarily opposed to the interests of the people. Direct democracy has no such disadvantages; it produces good government because wisdom necessarily gains ascendancy where there is widespread participation and open debate, and wise government always pursues the public good. But although direct democracy is sound in principle, it necessarily degenerates in practice; for good government leads to an expanding population, and large populations make direct democracies unworkable. The classical democracies degenerated into monarchical or aristocratic tyrannies as they expanded. Only representative government can combine the principles of direct democracy with any extent of territory or population. It is a system of government which is 'capable of embracing and confederating all the various interests' regardless of the size of the state (I. 371).

This formulation sounds similar to our modern conception of representative government as a means of aggregating and furthering the range of interests within a community. But this is misleading; for Paine retains the republican framework of analysis to the extent that he continues to see government as at best a necessary evil, as something which threatens the liberty and security of citizens by the exercise of arbitrary power, and as legitimate only when directed to the common good. Representative government is valued by Paine only in so far as it ensures that no special interests are pursued by government. This condition is met when wisdom and virtue rule and exercise power to the public good. Although he occasionally speaks of law as the expression of the general will (II. 546), he does not believe that

73

rule by representatives is a direct expression of popular sovereignty. He holds the less confident view that representation is a trust, and that the actions of representatives and the laws passed by them may or may not conform to the general will. Indeed, most of Paine's discussion of representative government is taken up with arguments about which particular mechanisms are most likely to ensure that this trust is not abused. Frequent elections and periodic recourse to conventions of the people set up to evaluate and reform the Constitution help keep representatives to their task, while division of the legislature during debates, so that representatives can weigh matters carefully and calmly, helps ensure that decisions are not made precipitately. The requirement that all laws be reviewed regularly, while motivated in part by Paine's position regarding the rule of one generation over those subsequent to it (which requires that each new generation has the opportunity to consent to or dissent from laws passed by its predecessors), is in part designed to ensure that government conforms to the present wisdom of the nation. But although the case is not pressed in the *Rights of Man*, Paine's French writings show his unequivocal commitment to the view that the greatest safeguard against arbitrary government is universal suffrage.

A government elected by only a section of the people has only that section's interests at heart, and inevitably deviates from the pursuit of the public good. Moreover, refusing a man (although apparently, and absurdly, not a woman) the right to vote 'implies stigma on the moral character of the persons excluded [which] no part of the community has a right to pronounce upon any other part' (II. 579). Liberty can be preserved only by giving each person an equal right in the exercise of power; for to deprive a man of the right to vote reduces him to the status of a slave, since 'slavery consists in being subject to the will of another, and he that has not a vote in the election of representatives is in this case' (II. 579). (Paine's willingness to deny women the vote, although understandable in the historical context, is indefensible. While he suggests that the only form of natural inequality is that between the sexes, it is inconceivable that he would accept the logic of his own argument, which suggests that they are natural slaves!) Paine further contends that having a right to vote imposes on a person a duty to obey. The converse also holds true: 'It is possible to exclude men from the right of voting, but it is impossible to exclude them from the right of rebelling against that exclusion; and when all other rights are taken away the right of rebelling is made perfect' (II. 580). (Women may take heart from this suggestion!) Property-based franchises are iniquitous: they are arbitrary, in that wealth and wisdom are not necessarily related; they are divisive, because they empower one part of the community to pursue its interests at the expense of the rest; and they are unjust, because the liberty of a person does not consist entirely in the right to protection of his property, but lies more fundamentally in the right to protection of his person. Paine also argues that the capacity to labour is itself a property, as significant as any other form of property and as much a basis for claiming a right to representation and enfranchisement (II.581).

The central problem for representative democracies is the possibility of a conflict of interests between the people and their governments. Such conflicts occur when particular individuals, groups, or classes gain privileged access to political power and use it to further their own ends. But in the absence of such corruption, the interests which the people have in common will always be much greater than those which divide them. In modern pluralist theories of representative government, governments respond to, aggregate, and sometimes promote the particular interests of the various sectors and associations of society. This view is anathema to Paine. He repeatedly denounces the influence of faction and party in government. Representation is to serve other ends: each individual must be represented so as to protect the equal rights of all. Within this framework of equal rights, government is directed by majority rule. But again, Paine's understanding of the majority principle is influenced by the republican tradition: thus majority rule means rule by the force of argument. Majority decisions are not automatically right; it does not follow from the fact that a majority prefers a particular policy that that policy is the best. The majority principle has the inherent virtue of being an unambiguous decision-procedure, but it produces good results only where the majority of the people are able to recognize the common good. But Paine departs from the republican tradition in his confidence in the wisdom of the people. Thus, 'in every land throughout the universe the tendency of the interest of the greatest number is in the direction of good rather than of evil, and the inevitable result must be to elevate the science of government to a height of perfection of which we have now no conception' (II. 531). The public good is determined by reason and experience, not by weight of numbers. Majority rule and representation are simply the safest way of ensuring that governments identify with the interests of the people as a whole. There is no area of government in which particular interests can legitimately contest for public power. *Society* is the arena for the pursuit of individual interests through the harmonizing system of commerce; *government's* minimal role is to protect this system and the equal rights of citizens, it is not intended to participate in it. The weight of Paine's argument for government and representation lies in the account he gives of society and the integrative effects of commerce:

It is to the great and fundamental principles of society and civilisation . . . to the unceasing circulation of interest, which, passing through its million channels, invigorates the whole mass of civilised man—it is to these things, infinitely more than to any thing which even the best constituted government can perform, that the safety and prosperity of the individual and the whole depends. The more perfect civilisation is, the less occasion it has for government. [I. 358–9]

This may sound utopian or naïve to our ears, but Paine's frequent references to the United States, to its form of government, conventions, and constitutions, and to its manifest virtues, demonstrates to his readers that his arguments are grounded in practical experience. America supports his account of the legitimate method for constituting governments, and shows that a society can be governed in such a manner. Part Two depicts America as the ideal towards which France is moving and to which Britain would also aspire were she not restrained by a corrupt court and a conniving aristocracy. But Paine's readers should not doubt the eventual outcome: 'I do not believe that monarchy and aristocracy will continue seven years longer in any of the enlightened countries of Europe. If better reasons can be shown for them than against them, they will stand; if the contrary they will not' (I. 352). And later: 'The present age will hereafter merit to be called the Age of Reason, and the present generation will appear to the future as the Adam of a new world' (I. 449). The references to America underline both that the republican system is desirable and that it is within his audience's grasp. For the common man in the 1790s, Paine's *Rights of Man* would not have sounded utopian—on the contrary, it might well have seemed an eminently practical possibility.

The cause of revolution

Paine's new account of the development of 'universal civilisation' has substantial implications for his theory of revolution. His earlier analysis of revolutionary change is common enough for the time: revolution is a Lockian act of resistance to political authorities which violate their trust by acting arbitrarily towards their citizens; it is thus a return to the principles of the founding contract of civil society. Some of Paine's comments on the French Revolution are in this vein; however, a rather different conception is also at work. Thus his insistence that the French Revolution was directed 'not against Louis XVI, but against the despotic *principle* of the government' should be understood as part of his new conception that an enlightened citizenry develops alongside an increase and a spread of commerce within and between nations. People see their interests more clearly, and are no longer susceptible to rule by imposture. As we have seen, this development is not explained solely in terms of the inevitable march of reason through the world. The representative democracies which will replace the European despotisms are certainly more rational systems; but Paine also tries to indicate the economic and social forces which have exposed the irrationality of the old order and which fuel the demands for a government directed by men of wisdom and virtue and based on the defence of the natural and civil rights of man. The result is an account of revolutions as progressive political changes arising from developments in the social and economic infrastructure of societies. Not only is this a relatively innovative, modern conception of revolution; it is also a far more plausible theory of social and political change than Paine is usually credited with.

Although this deeper theory is more often implied than made explicit, in *Decline and Fall of the English System of Finance* (1796) Paine does give a full and sophisticated analysis of the deeper causal forces at work in revolution. The revolution in question is the one he predicts for Britain. His analysis starts from comments made by Richard Price and Adam Smith to the effect that the system by which the British government funded its national debt will ultimately lead to national bankruptcy. Smith believed that the accumulated debt from the succession of wars fought since 1688—which Paine saw as a direct consequence of the Hanoverian succession—would eventually place such a burden of interest payments on the nation that taxation would prove incapable of reducing the capital debt, even if it could meet the interest. Moreover, the high levels of taxation resulting from the debt would inevitably inhibit the development of productive capacity. In the end, Smith argued, governments heavily in debt would be forced to default on their payments or substantially to devalue their currency.

Although impressed by Smith's account, Paine believes that it can be extended. He thinks it is possible to show not just that bankruptcy will eventually result, but that there is a definite period of time beyond which the present system will not survive. His argument rests on French and American experiences of systems of public credit and paper money. Each country issued paper money (continental currency in the United States and assignats in France) to the full value of its debts. In each, this led to rapid inflation, because the supply of money so greatly exceeded the amount required for circulation that the value of the notes fell. In each, paper currency glutted the market, and could not be exchanged at its face value. In Britain, by contrast, governments issued notes only to the value of the interest to be paid, not to the value of the capital sum of the debt. Were the capital sum (c. £400m) issued in notes, the value of the paper currency would collapse. By issuing notes to the value of the interest only (approximately 5 per cent of the total), the Government had avoided rapid inflation. But Paine's argument is that inflation has been deferred, not avoided. Assuming a 5 per cent rate of interest, he calculates that the rate of collapse for the English system will be one-twentieth of that experienced in America and France. 'The accumulation of paper money in England is in proportion to the accumulation of interest upon every new loan; and therefore the progress to the dissolution is twenty times slower than if the capital were to be emitted and put into circulation immediately' (II. 654).

He also claims that there is a ratio which determines the rate at which the national debt (which arises almost entirely from foreign wars) expands. The English court engaged in six foreign wars between 1688 and 1796. At the end of the first, the national debt amounted to £21.5m. By 1796, 3 years into the sixth, it was fast approaching £400m. Paine believes that the debt increases at a rate of half as much again in the course of each war, and that this rate is, in effect, a Newtonian law of economics: thus a declining financial system and its government follow the same kind of inductively generated laws as falling bodies. The explanation for this law lies with the value and the amount of paper currency. As more and more paper money is issued, so the purchasing power of money is diminished while its face value is left intact. Thus, while the real costs of wars remain about the same, the inflationary effect of using paper currency to pay interest on the debt means that the face value of each new loan increases. Moreover, each new loan adds further to the amount of paper money in circulation, so the size of the debt necessarily spirals. Paine calculates the devaluation of the currency by 1796 to have been of the order of 8:1, this being the ratio at which French assignats stood a year earlier, just prior to their complete collapse in February 1796. The most that can be expected for England, then, is that its system of finance will last twenty years, taking into account the slower rate of decline resulting from issuing notes to the value of the interest only. The end will come in a flight from paper into gold and silver. In America and France, where the equivalence of paper and specie was not practised, the run on the banks was not fatal. In Britain, where the system depends on their equivalence, it will be. The Government will have to suspend payment on notes, which will result in a fiscal crisis which in turn will lead to a partial or total revolution in government. For Paine, *'public credit is suspicion asleep'* (II. 622). Once awakened, the distrust will abate only when the system of government which has perpetrated the frauds used to support these wars is swept aside.

Paine's analysis has a number of weaknesses: he fails to take into account the effects of increasing productivity and national income in assessing the country's capacity to support the debt; he assumes that the real cost of wars is relatively invariable; and he believes that suspension of specie payments would definitively prove the bankruptcy of the entire political system to the people of England. Yet, for all its flaws, the theory is hardly absurd. Its premisses were not uncommon in the period, as can be seen from Smith's work, and its conclusions are argued coherently. Moreover, it dovetails neatly with Paine's account of the bellicose character of monarchical rule. As commerce has developed, so kings have been able to sustain their foreign wars only by incurring substantial national debts. Exacting the punitively high rates of taxation required to support a war with ready cash can be expected to lead to unrest and to flight of capital from the country, thereby necessitating higher-interest loans. The system of commerce and banking which supports the debt thus provides short-term support for the European courts' quests for dominion and hegemony; but in the long term, as wars proliferate, the debts spiral out of control, and the seeds of fiscal and legitimation crises are sown. Its limitations notwithstanding, the theory remains a shrewd one.

The pamphlet is also a brilliant piece of polemic, which strikes hard at the central pillar of Pitt's administration. Pitt had succeeded in suppressing the main forces of radicalism in the country through the 'Gagging Acts' of 1795, the repeated suspension of habeas corpus, and the inauguration of what Charles James Fox called a 'Reign of Terror' against radicals and their Whig sympathizers (AG 390). By such means he had been able to keep control in a country which in 1795 and 1796 was demanding 'peace and bread' and which in 1797 faced a succession of naval mutinies. But no government can rely solely on repression. Without the support of the country's financial and political élite, Pitt's administration would have fallen, probably along with much else, for it depended on public credit—that is, on the public's confidence and on its money. What Paine seeks to do is to shake the confidence of British financiers. He uses arguments and assumptions which were common at the time in financial circles, and plays on existing fears that the national debt will bankrupt the country. He aims, at the very least, to make it more difficult for the government to borrow, thereby weakening Britain's position in the war; at best, for a run on the banks. The pamphlet attempts to make a run on the banks inevitable by making it *seem* inevitable. Regardless of whether we are willing to credit (or blame) Paine for the banking crisis of February 1797, we should acknowledge that he recognized a major area of weakness in the British financial system. Had the run occurred two years earlier, amidst the food, crimp, and anti-war riots of 1795, the war with France might well have been abandoned; and it is unlikely that Pitt would have retained the confidence of the general public or the political and financial élite.

Revolutionary violence

Although Paine certainly deserves the title of revolutionary, he was never comfortable with the use of violence for revolutionary ends. The new order is to rest on the harmony of men's interests, on reason, and on the defence of the rights of man, and it can be introduced only when public opinion is equal to it. Writing in 1787, Paine says:

Were government to offer freedom to the people, or to show an anxiety for that purpose, the offer would probably be rejected . . . the desire must originate with, and proceed from the mass of people, and when the impression becomes universal, and not before, is the important moment for the most effectual consolidation of national strength and greatness that can take place. [II. 634]

However, as the Revolution developed, Paine recognized that those who make revolutions necessarily lead opinion rather than simply reflect it; thus, 'It is never to be expected in a revolution that every man is to change his opinion at the same moment.' Indeed, he accepts that leaders of revolutions, motivated by the thirst for justice and liberty, may

permit to themselves a *discretionary exercise of power* regulated more by circumstance than by principle, which, were the practice to continue, liberty would never be established, or if established would soon be overthrown. . . . There never yet was any truth or any principle so irresistibly obvious that all men believed it at once. [II. 587]

But his point here is to restrain revolutionary actions, not to justify them.

Time and reason must co-operate with each other to the final establishment of any principle; and therefore those who may happen to be first convinced have not a right to persecute others, on whom conviction operates more slowly. The moral principle of revolutions is to instruct, not to destroy. [II. 587]

In *Agrarian Justice*, where he also identifies a potential disjunction between revolutionary government and the 'state of civilisation' in the nation, he again insists that a revolution in 'civilisation' can occur only if all citizens are guaranteed their natural, civil, and social rights.

The truly revolutionary government treats its citizens as equals by assuring their rights, and thereby wins their allegiance. Only where rights are unequal does insurrection occur (II. 588). A representative government, elected through universal suffrage and committed to the preservation of rights, has no place for violence. France's error was to declare a revolutionary government in October 1793—'a thing without either principle or authority' (II. 588)—and to leave herself without a properly constituted form of power. The ensuing terror was a government of the will of a faction, not a government of principle. Moreover, just as the American Revolution and the establishment of its Constitution should stand as an example of the true principles of revolution, so must the French Revolution stand as a warning against the potential of tyranny to assume a revolutionary guise (cf. II. 683).

The welfare of the people

Paine's confidence in the peaceful, harmonious system of commerce, his vigorous defence of the natural and civil rights of man, and his demands for minimal government seem to commit him to a *laissez-faire* or even a libertarian conception of government. Yet throughout his work he shows a deep concern for the poor in society, and does not doubt that governments have considerable responsibilities to them. While he shares this concern with his socialist successors, he differs by identifying the root cause of distress in the political, rather than the economic, system. The excessive taxation, particularly on commodities, levied to support the luxury and expense of profligate and bellicose courts and the concentration of wealth in the hands of a few, which results from primogeniture and court patronage, have reduced millions to an unnecessary poverty such that the fruits of their labour are insufficient to support them. In *Common Sense* he emphasizes how much wealthier in real terms, and therefore how much better preserved from want, the poor of America are by comparison with their counterparts in Europe. He also suggests that inequalities are a natural result of men's different capacities. He expands this latter comment in a later pamphlet on France:

> That property will ever be unequal is certain. Industry, superiority of talents, dexterity of management, extreme frugality, fortunate opportunities, or the opposite, or the means of those things will ever produce that effect, without ever having recourse to the harsh ill-sounding names of avarice and oppression; and besides this there are some men who, though they do not despise wealth, will not stoop to the drudgery or the means of acquiring it . . . while in others there is an avidity to obtain it by every means not punishable. [II. 580]

Nevertheless, alongside this view, with its implicit acceptance of the principle of free exchange, he develops, in his *Rights of Man* and *Agrarian Justice*, detailed proposals for a system of public welfare and social insurance financed by progressive taxation. This taxation is explicitly designed to limit the accumulation of personal property. These proposals and arguments give substances to Paine's ideal of a society ruled by the representative system; but they also show that his conception of property rights has changed substantially since his earlier works.

Paine's proposals for a system of welfare in Part Two are one aspect of his account of how a newly formed representative government would manage Britain's financial affairs. He assumes that the Court, with its extravagant spending, will be abolished, and that Britain will form an alliance with France and America which will allow them to pool their military resources and cut the costs of the standing army and naval establishments. By these measures alone, current government expenditure (leaving aside servicing of

the national debt) might be reduced from *c*. £7.5m to £1.5m
(which is still six times the sum expended by the American
government). Rather than cutting taxation by £6m, Paine
proposes a series of welfare expenditures, combined with a
reform of the taxation system. The existing poor-rates,
levied by the parishes, which place a particularly heavy
burden on families of moderate means, are to be replaced by
a national system of poor-relief financed by taxation. A sum
of £4m (twice that spent by the parishes) would be spent on
a variety of benefits, including a child benefit, paid only if
the child attends school 'to learn reading, writing and common arithmetic'; a supplementary benefit for the aged poor,
starting with an income supplement at age fifty, rising to a
full pension at sixty; a system of maternity and death
grants; and education for all those in need. There would
still be sufficient money left to fund accommodation and
employment for the casual poor of London. The remaining
£2m would provide compensation for disbanded sailors and
soldiers and wage increases for those remaining in service.
As the number of disbanded persons decreased through
death, taxation on basic commodities such as hops, soap,
and candles could be reduced. A further £0.5m of income
could be sacrificed by striking out the window taxes under
the Acts of 1766 and 1779, while the remaining £1m would
be kept in reserve.

Paine then turns his attention to reform of the taxation
system. He focuses on Pitt's Commutation Tax Act of
1784, which aimed to reduce smuggling and to increase
revenue by cutting the very high taxes on tea imports and
increasing the tax on windows. Pitt assumed that those
who drank a lot of tea were the sort of people who lived in
houses with a lot of windows! What Paine proposes in its
place is a property tax. Since the commutation tax was
aimed at luxuries, and since an income of £1,000 per
annum was a luxury, being more than sufficient to support
a family, Paine argues that incomes above this figure should

be taxed like any other luxury. The tax he proposes is directed against income from large, personal, inherited estates, not income from labour. It would be progressive, from 3*d*. in the pound on the first £500 to 100 per cent on incomes over £23,000. Such a tax would put the burden where it can be borne most easily, and would encourage the division of large estates among the children of landowners, thereby helping to end the inequitable system of primogeniture. Paine also believes that it would help curtail the corrupt influence exerted by those with land at elections. Although the detailed proposals on taxation which Paine advances in Part Two appear to run counter to his earlier willingness to see the market as the appropriate mechanism for determining distributions, he makes no real attempt to justify these radical incursions on property rights. Only in *Agrarian Justice* does he offer a defence of the State's right to intervene in private property holdings. There he gives two accounts, which together amount to a very modern conception of social justice.

In the first account he notes that if one effect of what is 'proudly, perhaps erroneously, called civilisation' is great affluence, another is wretchedness: 'The most affluent and the most miserable of the human race are to be found in the countries that are called civilised' (I. 610). Instead of consistently extolling the benefits of civilization, as he does in his *Letter to the Abbé Raynal* and the *Rights of Man*, he argues here that civilization creates poverty. While the natural state lacks the advantages which flow from agriculture, the arts, the sciences, and manufactures, it also lacks poverty. Civilization has made 'one part of society more affluent, and the other more wretched, than would have been the lot of either in a natural state' (ibid.). This is because civilization involves a transition from common, inclusive property rights to fixed, exclusive property rights—from land being held in common to private landed property. Since this development allows the land to be used much more productively—with Locke, he maintains that it can support something like ten times the population this way—we cannot return to the natural state. He also accepts, with Locke, that it is labour which turns inclusive into exclusive rights. However, he recognizes that the labour argument is itself in part responsible for the creation of poverty, since in deriving exclusive rights from inclusive rights plus labour, the value of the land becomes conflated with the values of the labour; and 'it is the value of the improvement only, and not the earth itself, that is individual property' (I. 611). Poverty develops because the poor do not have access to land and have no claim on those who now own it. On Paine's argument it is plain that every proprietor of cultivated land owes a ground-rent to the community for the land which he holds. Although cultivation improves the productivity of the land and allows a larger population to be sustained, the natural right to use of the earth remains intact. This natural right does not entitle everyone to an equal share of the profits made from the exclusive use of land, since much of the profit is the product of individual labour, which is the labourer's by right. But it does justify a form of compensation to 'all those who have been thrown out of their natural inheritance by the introduction of landed property' (I. 612). The compensation should be such that no person is in a worse condition when born into a state of civilization than he would have been if born into a state of nature. Moreover, it should be paid 'by subtracting from property a portion equal in value to the natural inheritance it has absorbed' (I. 613). He then details a proposal for a fund financed by death duties to pay all individuals a sum in lieu of their natural inheritance and to provide for the aged, the sick, and the infirm.

Paine's second argument takes the whole issue substantially further by including both landed property and personal wealth and income in his calculations. He admits that his first argument justifies a tax only on the former, but claims that the inclusion of personal property is justified by a different principle. Personal property, he argues, is 'the *effect of society* . . ., [for] separate the individual from society, and give him an island or a continent to possess, and he cannot acquire personal property'.

> All accumulation, therefore, of personal property, beyond what a man's own hands can produce, is derived to him by living in society; and he is owed on every principle of justice, of gratitude, and of civilisation, a part of that accumulation back again to society from whence the whole came. [I. 620]

Far from trying to explain inequality without recourse 'to the harsh, ill-sounding names of avarice and oppression', Paine now argues that in many cases the accumulation of personal property is the result of paying too little for the labour which produced it, 'the consequence of which is that the working hand perishes in old age, and the employer abounds in affluence' (ibid.; cf. II. 579). He does not insist on the exploitative nature of the labour contract, however, being content to make the more conciliatory but equally corrosive claim that it is impossible 'to proportion exactly the price of labour to the profit it produces' (I. 620). Given this, and assuming that even if the full fruits of labour were paid to the labourer, he might not be able to save enough to guard against hardship in old age, it makes sense that society should act as a treasurer for him.

But there is a further argument at work here. Paine believes that the extremes of poverty and affluence in civilized society are clear evidence of injustice, and that the injustice is compounded over time. 'The great mass of the poor in all countries are become an hereditary race, and it is next to impossible for them to get out of that state themselves' (I. 619). Moreover, their numbers increase annually, generating class antagonism, which threatens the security of property and the stability of society. Only where the affluence of the few benefits their fellow citizens can such class antagonism be avoided; and only then will all citizens unite to ensure that property is secured and respected.

In part Paine's argument appeals to the prudence of the rich; in part it makes a broader appeal to social justice. Because wealth is the fruit of social co-operation, it is unjust that some should enjoy abundance while others are impoverished. The reciprocity which underpins society is violated just as much by this injustice as it is by the insurrectionary outbursts it may prompt. In Paine's view, where the poor are worse off than they would be in a state of nature, they owe nothing to the countries in which they live; and if they do not revolt, it is only because their spirit has been broken. Justice requires not absolute equality, which is neither possible nor desirable, but the maintenance of a bond of reciprocity and mutual interest between rich and poor such that property does not become a source of resentment and contention in society. Paine's proposed fund is designed to resolve such conflicts:

> When the riches of one man above another shall increase the national fund in the same proportion; when it shall be seen that the prosperity of the fund depends on the prosperity of individuals; when the more riches a man acquires, the better it shall be for the general mass; it is then that antipathies will cease, and property be placed on the permanent basis of national interests and protection. (I. 621)

Although it differs in both method and detail, Paine's argument in *Agrarian Justice* has much in common with that advanced by John Rawls in his *Theory of Justice* (1972). Rawls argues that a society is just when the distribution of rights, liberties, and social goods is governed by the following principles: (1) 'Each person is to have an equal right to the most extensive total system of equal basic liberties compatible with a similar system of liberty for all'; (2) 'Social and economic inequalities are to be arranged so that they are both (a) to the greatest benefit to the least advantaged and (b) attached to offices and positions open to all under conditions of fair equality of opportunity' (p. 83). The first principle has priority over the second, and (2b) has priority over (2a), which is known as the 'difference principle'. The details of Rawls's argument need not concern us here; but his two principles are useful because they provide a more precise formulation of Paine's general position. Paine holds that fundamental natural and civil rights are to be given absolute priority, since it is for their preservation that civil society is created. Equality of opportunity is also to be guaranteed: 'All citizens have the right of admission to all public positions, enjoyments and functions. The only motives for preference known to a free people are talents and virtues' (II. 559). A society in which inequalities of wealth interfere with the principle of equal opportunity is unjust, even if greater aggregate wealth is the result. Paine now sees landed property and personal wealth as the outcome of social co-operation, rather than something generated wholly by the natural right to the fruits of one's labour. Consequently, redistribution of such wealth by the State does not violate natural rights—indeed, it can be seen as a way of more fully respecting the fundamental rights of citizens. Paine's version of Rawls's difference principle is less stringent, but basically similar. The appropriation of wealth is just when it simultaneously increases proportionally the fund which provides the starting capital of £15 to each person arriving at the age of twenty-one and a pension to all those over fifty or suffering from an incapacitating debility. Early in the pamphlet Paine falls short of the difference principle by declaring that 'I care not how affluent some may be, provided that none be miserable in consequence of it' (I. 617). In his concluding comments, however, he implies a stronger version by arguing that 'when the more riches a man acquires, the better it shall be for the general mass; it is then that antipathies will cease, and property be placed on the more permanent basis of national interest and protection' (I. 621). Resentment of wealth which does not produce such benefits is not envy but an appropriate response to injustice.

The comparison with Rawls is instructive in two further ways. The first concerns Paine's implicit development of the principle of fair equality of opportunity as against his earlier commitment to the principle of 'careers open to talents'. Rawls distinguishes the two as follows. The latter requires that positions are formally open to all—that is, that there is no rule barring any class or group of individuals from competing for places. The former demands that persons with similar abilities and skills be given similar life chances. But the distribution of abilities is random, and where there is a hereditary class of poor, people with similar abilities do not have similar life chances. In *Agrarian Justice* Paine goes beyond the formal equality demanded by many of the *philosophes* (who used the principle to challenge aristocratic privilege on behalf of the rising middle classes) to a democratic equality which is conscious of the distortions which wealth can introduce. Paine does not develop the point at length, but his recognition of the problem is an important indication of his democratization of a central plank of *philosophe* thought.

The second further point at which the comparison with Rawls is useful concerns their shared view that a well-ordered, just society relies both on a mutual understanding of principles of justice and on a citizenry which sees beyond its immediate interests and is involved practically in the political institutions of its society. For both Paine and Rawls civilization involves not just the production of wealth, but the creation of a community in which the rights and particular interests of all are protected and in which political rule is regulated by a publicly shared conception of justice. That is why Paine insists, in *Dissertations on Government* (1786), that 'a republic, properly understood, is a sovereignty of justice, in contradistinction to a sovereignty of will' (II. 375). For both men, democracy and representative government are crucial mechanisms in the development of shared views of the duties of citizens and in the maintenance of a public life orientated to the pursuit of the public good, or a sovereignty of justice.

4 The Kingdom of Heaven

In the *Rights of Man* the right of conscience or religion is
described as a perfect natural right—that is, one 'where the
power to execute is as perfect in the individual as the right
itself' (I. 276). The power to exercise the right is perfect
because each human being has the capacity to reason and
to form beliefs about the existence and nature of the Deity
and the duties owed thereto. However, although there are
comments on God, Providence, and religion scattered
throughout Paine's political writings, these do not add up
to a coherent statement of Paine's religious beliefs. This
task is reserved for the third major work of his corpus, his
Age of Reason.

The grounds of belief

Part One of the *Age of Reason* relies on two basic axioms.
The first is that the Word of God is unchangeable and is
expressed in a universal language available to all equally—
'A thing which every one is required to believe requires that
the proof and evidence of it shall be equal to all, and
universal' (I. 468). No man or institution can claim
privileged access to the divine will; therefore what is
available as proof to one must be available as proof to all.
The only truly universal language is that expressed in the
design of the Creation, which the faculty of reason allows
us to comprehend. The second axiom is that true belief
derives from the exercise of reason and its handmaid probability. God speaks through his creation to this universal
faculty of reason, and thereby allows all to grasp his design
and to recognize their duties to him. Revelation is not an
alternative source of religious belief; it is acceptable only in
so far as it conforms to reason. It follows that the right of

conscience is a perfect natural right: we are each endowed with the faculty of reason, and no higher authority exists in matters of conscience than reason and common sense. 'My mind is my own church,' and the only form of infidelity is unfaithfulness to the teachings of this 'church'.

Paine's view that reason and common sense are touchstones for belief is evident in the way he presents his case. He approaches the Bible with a wilful disregard for his predecessors in biblical exegesis and deism. While this is partly out of ignorance, it is also in line with his insistence that what he writes should be intelligible to anyone brought up in the Christian tradition. He is offering a 'plain man's guide' to the Bible, not an attempt at biblical hermeneutics. This 'guide' is also a profession of faith: a faith, above all, in a reasonable God and a rational order to the universe, but also a faith that each person's common sense is sufficient to reach conclusions about the nature of the Deity which are as valid as those of the next person. The *Age of Reason* presents Paine's own conclusions, and uses them as the basis of an attack on the pretensions of the Christian churches to special authority in religious matters. Just as *Common Sense* and the *Rights of Man* laid the axe of reason to the tree of kingly corruption, force, and fraud, so the *Age of Reason* lays it to that other pillar of national superstition and imposture, the established Church. Indeed, Paine explicitly links the recent revolutions in government to that which he wishes to promote in religion: 'The adulterous connection between church and state' wherever it has existed has so repressed discussion of established creeds and first principles of religious belief that it has taken a revolution in France to bring these subjects out into the open. Once discussion is free, we can expect nothing less than a revolution in religion: 'Human inventions and priestcraft would be detected; and man would return to the pure, unmixed and unadulterated belief in one God and no more' (I. 465).

Paine

Paine's principal target in the *Age of Reason* is the
Christian churches' claims to authority in matters of belief.
Since these claims rest ultimately on the belief that the
Church has a special mission from God, revealed in the
Bible, he begins by denying the relevance of revelation. For
the sake of argument he supposes that God might choose
to speak directly to someone on earth; but even if this
did happen, it would be revelation to that person only.
Everyone else would have to rely on that person's report; it
would remain hearsay, 'and, consequently they are not
obliged to believe it' (I. 466). True belief must rest on the
evidence we find before us. As regards the story of the
Virgin Birth, we must try to gauge how likely it is to be true.
None of the key participants is available for questioning, so
we must rely on evidence and probability, which Paine find
insufficient to warrant belief. He goes further by claiming
that it is far more reasonable to believe that the story derives
from the heathen mythology which was fashionable at the
time. To their credit, the Jews, 'who had always rejected the
heathen mythology' never believed the story (I. 467).

All the stories in the Bible should be assessed in this way.
With regard to each, we should ask what external supporting evidence exists; then we should see what internal
evidence there is for its divine provenance. Having dismissed the account of Christ's conception and birth, Paine
goes on to apply these two methodological principles to the
whole of Christ's life as it is presented in the New Testament. The Resurrection and the Ascension are both given
short shrift, being regarded as nothing more than attempts
to spirit Christ from the earth in as supernatural a manner
as he is said to have come into it. The only evidence
available comes from a few people who 'are introduced as
proxies for the whole world to say they saw it, and all the
rest of the world are called upon to believe it' (I. 468). Paine
sides unequivocally with Thomas: he will not believe
it without 'having ocular and manual demonstration

himself'. This part of the story has 'every mark of fraud and imposture stamped upon the face of it'. There is no need to deny Christ's existence, however. That he existed and was crucified 'are historical relations strictly within the bounds of probability'. Indeed, as a 'virtuous reformer and revolutionist', he was in all likelihood killed as a result of a conspiracy between the Jews and their Roman rulers, both of whom were threatened by his preaching of equality and his attacks on priestly corruption (I. 469).

The internal evidence for Christ's divinity is also weak in Paine's view. Although the morality Christ preached and practised was of the most benevolent kind, it is not unlike that taught by Confucius and some of the Greek philosophers, and it has been preached by many good men in all ages; so it is not specifically Christian. Paine also denounces in the strongest terms the claim that Christ died for the sins of the world. To accept that is to think of God as a passionate, irrational man who kills his Son when he cannot be avenged on his creation in any other way (because of the self-denying ordinance taken after the flood) (I. 497). Moreover, he claims, the doctrine of redemption was fabricated only as a means of generating income for the Church by the selling of pardons, dispensations, and indulgences (I. 480–1). Paine does not doubt that the Church's assumed monopoly of redemption is wholly fraudulent, for 'man stands in the same relative condition with his Maker as he ever did stand since man existed (I. 481). Believing this allows people to 'live more consistently and more morally than by any other system'. Against this, the Christian Church teaches its faithful that they are no better than outlaws, outcasts, and beggars, 'who must make [their] approaches by creeping and cringing to intermediate beings' (I. 482–3). The man who is not driven to indifference to religion by this oppression turns devout, and surrenders the greatest of God's gifts:

. . . he consumes his life in grief, or the affectation of it; his prayers are reproaches; his humility is ingratitude; he calls himself a worm, and the fertile earth a dunghill; and all the blessings of life by the thankless name of vanities; he despises the choicest gift of God to man, the GIFT OF REASON; and having endeavoured to force upon himself the belief of a system against which reason revolts, he ungratefully calls it *human reason*, as if man could give reason to himself. [I. 482.]

The Old Testament receives even shorter shrift. The external evidence for its authenticity is said to be practically nil. The Church mythologists simply 'collected all the writings they could find and managed them as they pleased' (I. 472). They decided 'by *vote* which of the books out of the collection they had made should be the WORD OF GOD'. Some were rejected; some were styled the Apocrypha; and those supported by the majority were accepted as the Word of God. 'Had they voted otherwise, all the people since calling themselves Christians, had believed otherwise—for the belief of the one derives from the vote of the other' (I. 473). If this is the external authority of the Bible, then it is no authority at all! On the measure of internal evidence, the Old Testament fares even less well. It is a morass of superstition, mythology, and absurdity. Having followed Jupiter's example (confining Enceladus beneath Etna) by casting Satan into a pit, Christian mythologists are obliged to let him out again 'to bring on the sequel of the fable':

He is then introduced into the Garden of Eden, in the shape of a snake or a serpent, and in that shape he enters into familiar conversation with Eve, who is no way surprised to hear a snake talk; and the issue of this *tête-à-tête* is that he persuades her to eat an apple, and the eating of that apple damns all mankind. [I. 470]

Paine is not trying to be funny: he writes with a dark, bitter irony. The Church mythologists have woven a tale in which the Devil triumphs over creation, and in which, even after the sacrifice of Christ, he is still promised 'ALL the Jews, ALL the Turks by anticipation, nine-tenths of the world beside, and Mahomet into the bargain' (I. 470). In their account, Satan is omnipresent and seemingly omnipotent; for he defeats by strategy all the power and wisdom of the Almighty, who is forced either to surrender the whole of the creation to Satanic rule or to capitulate for its redemption 'by coming down upon the earth, and exhibiting Himself upon a cross in the shape of a man' (I. 471). The whole story defies rational belief. That it has survived is a tribute to the mendacity of the priesthood and the gullibility and ignorance of the people.

Paine also denies that the Old Testament contains 'revelation'. It is made up entirely of historical description and anecdote: 'When we contemplate the immensity of the being who directs and governs the incomprehensible whole . . . we ought to feel shame at calling such paltry stories the Word of God' (I. 473). But the strongest internal evidence against the Old Testament being the Word of God is its content:

> Whenever we read the obscene stories, the voluptuous debaucheries, the cruel and torturous executions, the unrelenting vindictivenesss, with which more than half the Bible is filled, it would be more consistent that we called it the word of a demon than the Word of God. It is a history of wickedness that has served to corrupt and brutalize mankind; and, for my part, I sincerely detest it as I detest everything that is cruel. [I. 474]

The only sections of the Old Testament for which Paine has any use are 'some chapters in Job and the 19th Psalm', which are 'true *deistical* compositions, for they treat the *Deity* through his works' (I. 484). For the most part, the rest does more harm than good.

The true revelation

To Paine it is obvious that the means used by God to accomplish his ends must be equal to the task. To communicate to mankind his power, munificence, and abundance, he must speak in the only language which is accessible to all—namely, the language of nature. 'It is only in the CREATION that all our ideas and conceptions of a *Word of God* can unite . . . it is an ever-existing original, which every man can read.' Moreover, 'it preaches to all nations and to all worlds; and this Word of God reveals to man all that it is necessary for man to know of God' (I. 483). Because 'everything we behold carries in itself the internal evidence that it did not make itself', we are forced to conclude that there must be a First Cause 'eternally existing, of a nature totally different to any material existence we know of, and by the power of which all things exist' (I. 484). It is this First Cause which we call God. Our belief in God is a deduction of reason, not a postulate of faith. Since reason is the only ground of true religious belief, it follows that the only true theology is natural philosophy, or science. Paine remains loyal to the Newtonianism he imbided at lectures given by Benjamin Martin and James Ferguson in London in the 1750s (I. ix and 496). Science discovers the principles and laws which govern the universe, and comes to recognize in part the divine plan upon which the universe is constructed. It reveals the true basis for religious belief, and undermines superstition and mythology and the claims to miracles and mysteries upon which the Church has built its power.

The *Age of Reason* is a confession of belief. Paine finds ample evidence of the power, wisdom, and munificence of the Deity in the immensity of the Creation, in 'the unchangeable order by which the incomprehensible [*sic*] whole is governed', and in the abundance of goods on earth. He celebrates the principles discovered by science which reveal the structure of the universe and provide the basis for the practical and applied sciences by which man imitates the divine order. Moreover, he conjectures that God designed the order of the heavens and made it visible to mankind so as to provide ample confirmation of its divine origin. He also argues for a plurality of worlds in the universe, maintaining that, just as our own world is crowded with life, so there is every reason to believe that there are many other inhabited planets. Our solar system occupies just a small portion of space, and what we see as fixed stars are probably the suns of other solar systems around which other worlds and planets revolve. This seems all the more probable given the benefits which would flow from this plurality. This complex whole stimulates scientific discovery and the mechanical sciences throughout the universe.

> The inhabitants of each of the worlds of which our system is composed enjoy the same opportunities of knowledge as we do. They behold the revolutionary motions of our earth, as we behold theirs. All the planets revolve in sight of each other and, therefore, the same universal school of science presents itself to us all. [I. 503]

Our ideas of God's attributes—his wisdom, beneficence, omnipotence, and so on—are enlarged as we contemplate this structure. Such contemplation also helps to undermine the Christian conceit that the Almighty 'who had millions dependent on his protection, should quit the care of all the rest, and come to die in our world, because, they say, one man and one woman had eaten an apple' (I. 504).

A further corollary of Paine's natural theology is an anticipated convergence of belief. Religion is a branch of science, a matter of reason, not faith. Consequently there can be only one true religion, only one which accords with the ever-existing Word of God. We may devise different ways of paying homage to him, but it remains the case that religious beliefs are fully cognitive.

From this 'true revelation', we can learn how best to live our lives. The Creation proclaims the power, the wisdom, and the beneficence of God; and 'the moral duty of man consists in imitating the moral goodness and beneficence of God, manifested in the creation towards all His creatures'. God's beneficence to humanity sets an example to all, and demonstrates that 'persecution and revenge between man and man, and everything of cruelty towards animals, is a violation of natural duty' (I. 512). Paine purports to be not much exercised by the manner of a future existence; but he does not doubt that his Maker could continue his existence should he please, and thinks it probable that a future state exists.

The first part of the *Age of Reason* was written without access to the Bible. Paine's admission of this fact drew ridicule from his critics, but benefited his arguments considerably. It forced him to adopt a style of argument which retains its power today. For the most part, his biblical references and allusions are immediately recognizable by readers with only the barest acquaintance with the Bible and the Christian tradition. To scholars and divines, his comments grossly over-simplify complex issues; but to the common reader schooled by parsons and preachers in a literal reading of the Old and New Testaments, the stories Paine refers to were a common cultural inheritance, accepted uncritically and ripe for challenge. Paine's attack, here as elsewhere, is not directed to the erudite but to the common reader, whom he buttonholes with both vigour and respect—vigour, in that he writes in a direct, forceful, and accessible manner; and respect, in that he treats his reader as a rational, reflective person, capable of recognizing that the private judgement of the individual is the only court of appeal in matters theological, as in matters political. We are to judge the Bible against standards of natural reason and humanitarian concern; where it asks us to accept as God's will something which violates these canons, we are advised to look for an explanation of these myths, rather than attributing to them the status of the Word of God. No great biblical learning is required; we must each form the best judgement we can.

This emphasis on the supreme authority of the individual's conscience is the strongest side of Paine's arguments; and it is here that he has most in common with his deist predecessors. It gains additional strength from its rationalism, as when it is combined with the Newtonian panegyric on the revelation to reason and science of the divinely ordered universe. But even without such rationalism, in a world in which assertions about laws of nature cannot command agreement, it remains a powerful case. There is still no more authentic form of belief than that generated by the unfettered exercise of the individual's understanding. Paine's commitment to rational religion presumes that in the absence of force and fraud there will be a convergence of belief and the emergence of a consensus. We may find this implausible, but this does not mean that we must accept the conservative position that a hierarchical State and an established Church are prerequisites for the maintenance of the social order and its attendant benefits. The people may not be as rational in their political or religious thinking as Paine anticipated, but he is surely right to insist that it is they who must judge.

The Age of Reason continued

The second and third parts of the *Age of Reason* are less easy to assess. Although Paine has had access to the Bible, he remains largely ignorant of existing critical work. Assured of the sufficiency of reason and common sense, he works methodically through the Bible so as to satisfy himself that he has not done it an injustice in Part One. Unsurprisingly he finds that his principal error was to speak better of some parts of the Bible than they deserve.

The tone of Part Two is set by his opening comment that the contents of the Bible are often 'as shocking to humanity and every idea we have of moral justice as anything done by Robespierre [*et al.*]' (I. 518). They so violate our natural conceptions of God's justice and benevolence that we need to be doubly satisfied as to the reliability of those who testify that God ordered such things. The outcome of this inquiry is never really in doubt:

> . . . to read the Bible without horror, we must undo everything that is tender, sympathizing and benevolent in the heart of man. Speaking for myself, if I had no other evidence that the Bible is fabulous than the sacrifice I must make to believe it to be true, that alone would be sufficient to determine my choice. [I. 519]

But in the interests of objectivity, Paine postpones this conclusion, and the bulk of Part Two is devoted to undermining the authority of the testimony which the Bible represents as the authentic Word of God.

He sets out to prove that many of the books of the Bible simply could not have been written by the authors to whom they are ascribed—for example, the book of Joshua. Likewise there is sufficient textual evidence and historical corroboration to demonstrate that the Pentateuch was not written by Moses. The author uses the third person, and praises Moses' humility, which means that if Moses was the author, he was also 'one of the most vain and arrogant of coxcombs' (I. 522). In the case of Deuteronomy, the dramatical style and the interchange of speakers suggest that Moses was not the author; further, there are references to the death and burial of Moses and turns of phrase which suggest that the writer is describing events long past. Moreover, the references in Genesis 14:14 to Abraham pursuing the captors of Lot to Dan run directly counter to references to Dan in Judges 18: 27–9. In the latter it is said that the town was formerly Laish, and that it was renamed Dan only when it was invaded by the tribe of that name, which wished to commemorate the father of the tribe, the great-grandson of Abraham; so the town was not renamed Dan until some three hundred years after Moses' death. Using the same method he shows that some of Genesis was written after the time of David, and that the text is often directly paralleled in some of the later books of the Bible.

He brings a similar case against the books of Joshua and Samuel, and says of Judges, on account of the anonymity of its author, that it has 'not so much as a nominal voucher' for its authenticity. As for Ruth,

> it is an idle, bungling story, foolishly told, nobody knows by whom, about a strolling country-girl, creeping slyly to bed with her cousin Boaz. Pretty stuff indeed, to be called the Word of God. It is however, one of the best books in the Bible, for it is free of murder and rapine. [I. 535]

The later books of the Old Testament and those of the New are handled with similar gusto. The only book to escape unscathed is Job, although, following Spinoza and Abenezra, he argues that it is not originally a Hebrew but a Gentile work.

Paine's argument throughout is that the authority of the Bible rests on the validity of the testimony it contains, and that this authority necessarily evaporates under scrutiny, since the testimony is found to be anonymous and contradictory. Most of Paine's critics and most modern Christians reject this logic. It is now agreed, for example, that the Pentateuch is a compilation from a variety of sources. Paine's argument concerning Dan is widely accepted, and a good many of his comments concerning inconsistencies, varying styles, omissions, and so on would not have been out of place—suitably toned down—in scholarly discussions of his day. Yet such scholarly considerations have not persuaded Christians to abandon Christianity in favour of deism. Many of Paine's critics were prepared to concede on some issues without thereby conceding all. It seems, then, that Paine's attack misfired—perhaps doubly so, since little he says had not been said by his precursors in the deist controversy of the first half of the eighteenth century— Matthew Tindal, Thomas Chubb, Anthony Collins, and Conyers Middleton. Yet Paine's account is shrewder and more powerful than appears at first blush.

Consider, for example, Bishop Richard Watson's attempted rebuttal, *An Apology for the Bible*. Watson uses two arguments which seem to strike at the heart of Paine's case, in that they attack the sufficiency of natural reason and the view that natural standards of justice exist against which the morality of the Scriptures may be measured. He insists that conscience cannot stand as an authoritative voice of natural law, because it is shaped and given content by education and social experience. He also claims that the killing of the children of the Canaanites, which so appalled Paine, is no more a contradiction of the moral justice of God than are natural disasters such as earthquakes. But Watson's case is not strong. It is not a good strategy to appeal to the weakness of reason to support claims that certain beliefs must be valid! Watson's arguments may show that the rigorous searching of conscience and the exercise of reason cannot produce objective standards or beliefs, but they do not provide us with *reasons* for believing in God and scriptural authority. Watson's arguments are sceptical, even if they are accompanied by appeals to his readers to trust in the established authorities and to have faith that the Scriptures do in fact contain the revealed Word of God. But reason cannot justify either the trust or the faith. For all the appearance of reasonableness which marks Watson's style, his ultimate appeal is to his readers' willingness to have faith and to follow the authority and traditions of the Church.

Watson's account simply does not engage the thrust of

Paine's argument. When he pleads, 'Do but grant that the Supreme Being communicated to any of the sons of men a knowledge of future events, so that their predictions were plainly verified, and you will find little difficulty in admitting the truth of revealed religion' (*Apology* 134), he is refusing to recognize that Paine's case goes to the heart of such claims. Any particular revelation is hearsay, and biblical reports of it are equally uncertain. To command belief, revelation must have such unimpeachable authority that its falsity is less probable than its truth—which is a tall order given that in most cases revelation goes against everything we know of the world. Anything which casts doubt on the authorship of the Bible increases the probability that claims to revelation are forgeries. Even if Watson's negative arguments against reason are accepted, all that follows is that whatever we believe, we must take on trust; but this is not a *reason* for preferring one set of beliefs over another—for example, theism to deism. Indeed, Watson's case is weakened still further when he acknowledges that some of Paine's specific points may be valid. For, while he rightly says that the inauthenticity of a few phrases does not mean that everything contained in the Bible is thereby inauthentic, he cannot provide a rational criterion for distinguishing between authentic and inauthentic sections of the Bible. He can only encourage us to draw the line where Church authorities tell us we should—but they have no reason for preferring one way to another. Paine's negative case against the Bible is more powerful than Watson's negative case against reason, because Paine establishes (as Watson concedes) that belief in the Scriptures cannot be unconditional. Watson takes faith and Church tradition as authoritative diviners of valid testimony, whereas Paine sees faith as a legacy from a more superstitious age, and offers reason and probability as alternatives. Even if Paine's positive case for natural reason cannot be sustained, his attack on the Bible remains corrosive because it reveals the non-rational character of Christian belief, which he sees as involving assertion against assertion, superstition against superstition. Although much of Part Two is laboured, it remains a shrewd commentary on the claim that Christianity can be reasonable. (Part Three does essentially the same, focusing on New Testament references to Old Testament prophecies.)

That Paine's arguments are not original is likewise not particularly damaging. His originality lies less in what he says than in how he says it and to whom. While he covers much the same ground as the deists in the earlier controversy, he does so before a new audience—new, partly because the controversy went underground after the 1750s, leaving the Church to reassert the old dogmas, and partly because many of the readers of the *Age of Reason* would not have followed the earlier controversy. Paine's work was read by a new generation and by a much broader public, including the lower orders, than had been reached by the earlier controversy, which had raged only among the educated and well-to-do members of a patrician culture. Its eclipse came in the 1750s, when the public ethos became more tolerant of the various manifestations of dissent and the establishment less biblically aggressive. However, as Leslie Stephen has noted, the long-term outcome of the deist controversy seems to have been to generate an essentially sterile orthodox theology, one suited to 'absentee bishops and professors of divinity, perfunctorily treading their mill-wheel round of duty' (LS I. 391), and one which relied on a comfortable, but essentially non-spiritual, consensus. By the end of the eighteenth century the hold of the established Church over the common people had become increasingly insecure. On the one hand, the evangelical religions were gaining new members; on the other, rationalism, deism, and atheism were spreading. Either way, it was becoming increasingly apparent to many that the Anglican Church could satisfy neither their spiritual needs nor the demands of reason. And it was Paine's *Age of Reason* which, more than any other work in the last quarter of the eighteenth century, made the latter clear. Indeed, it is here that the key to Paine's success, and to much of his subsequent infamy, lies. Faced with an increasingly moribund orthodoxy, the artisan classes were ripe for revolt against establishment dogmas, and the *Age of Reason* provided them with a new, virulent confirmation of the theological, and hence moral, bankruptcy of the established Church.

> Paine's book announced a startling fact, against which all the flimsy collections of conclusive proofs were powerless. It amounted to a proclamation that the creed no longer satisfied the instincts of rough common sense any more than the intellects of cultivated scholars. When the defenders of the old orders tried to conjure with the old charms, the magic had gone out of them. In Paine's rough tones they recognised not the mere echo of coffee-house gossip, but the voice of deep popular passion. Once and for ever, it announced that, for the average mass of mankind, the old creed was dead. [LS I. 391]

Deism and morality

The *Age of Reason* stands up well as an attack on the dogmas of orthodox Christian belief in so far as that belief purports to be reasonable. But the Christian Church was only one of Paine's targets. The other was atheism. With regard to the former, his case was predominantly negative, and his challenge of the reasonableness of Christianity was not overly weakened by attacks on his rationalism. But his positive case depends entirely on the claim that belief in a single Deity is a deduction of reason. Some assessment of the strength of this argument must be made, not because it will necessarily tell us very much about how persuasive Paine's contemporaries found him, but because, in so far as Paine's political theory can be shown to rely heavily on ethical principles derived from his deism, weaknesses in the latter will have major implications for our understanding and evaluation of his entire corpus.

There does seem to be a prima-facie case for thinking that Paine's religious convictions underlie his moral philosophy. It is not difficult to see that Paine's deism helps to explain both our natural tendency towards society and how our natural sympathies and affections lead us to recognize our moral duties to others. It also helps to turn hypothetical into categorical claims: on the one hand, it explains why we all have these sentiments (God has given us a common nature); on the other, even in the absence of such feelings, it establishes our duty as rational agents subject to God's authority to improve the happiness of his creation.

Moreover, as we have seen, Paine's account of the rights of individuals falls back on theist premisses; thus, 'If we proceed on, we shall at last come out right; we shall come to the time when man came from the hand of his Maker' (I. 273). It is God's creation of us as equals—and the right he has to set rules for us (a right, following Locke, derived from the act of creation)—which grounds natural-rights claims. Further, it is by inductive reasoning about God's intentions for his creation that we can derive a list of those rights which ought to be recognized and defended for each individual.

For Paine, religion encompasses both 'the belief of a God and the practice of moral truth' (I. 506). The former follows naturally and necessarily from contemplating the complex design of the universe. The latter involves 'a practical imitation of the goodness of God', which means 'our acting toward each other as he acts benignly to all' (ibid.). Paine sees this as requiring that we help others, but without losing sight of our own happiness. The rewards for doing so are evident—at least to Paine:

My own opinion is that those whose lives have been spent in doing good and endeavouring to make their fellow mortals happy—for this is the only way in which we can serve God—*will be happy hereafter*; and that the very wicked will meet with some punishment. But those who are neither good nor bad, or are not too insignificant [*sic*] for notice, will be dropped entirely. This is my opinion. It is consistent with my idea of God's justice, and with the reason God has given me; and I gratefully know that he has given me a large share of that gift. [PT 123]

Yet, despite Paine's confidence, his account of the intimate connection between belief in God and the nature of our moral duties is actually very weak. There is no way of deducing from the existence of God the rule that one ought to live the kind of life which Paine aspired to lead. If we accept Christian teachings, we have no such difficulties, since the will of God as revealed in the Bible can be used to generate a fairly complex picture of our moral rights and obligations. But without this supporting apparatus, the postulate of a rational deity simply cannot do the work which Paine evidently thought it could.

The task is simpler if we rely on the motives for moral action provided by an afterlife; but this not only invokes a more pusillanimous version of morality than he normally admits, it also relies on a postulate which is more a matter of faith than reason. *Contra* Paine, we have no rational grounds for believing in an afterlife or for ascribing to that life one character rather than another; or, indeed, for imagining that one sort of behaviour will get us there, whereas another will not. It is true that if we postulate a rational and just God, we might be able to say something about the criteria for admission to an afterlife which he might use. But it would hardly be irrational for there to be no afterlife; nor would it be irrational for everyone to be admitted to whatever kind of afterlife there might be. Similarly, Paine's category of 'also-rans'—an uncharacteristically élitist touch—is hardly compelling. The category might be excused as a side-swipe at a Church whose morality Paine saw as inhumanly complacent in the face of the poverty and hardship of many of its flock; but it is quite clear that it is not a logical deduction from God's 'benignity'.

Paine's arguments for the existence of God are also inadequate. He combines two popular eighteenth-century accounts: the First Cause argument and the argument from design. He expresses the former so badly that it looks as if he has committed the simple logical fallacy of assuming that since everything is caused by something, some thing must be the cause of everything, that 'some-thing' being God. He also argues that, 'incomprehensible and difficult as it is for man to conceive what a first cause is', it is ten times more difficult not to believe in one (I. 484). This is sheer assertion. The existence of God is no more rationally compelling a solution to the problem of the regression of causes than is the idea that causes regress to infinity. Within existing canons of rational inquiry, it is no more extraordinary to regard the universe as a freak event than it is to postulate the existence and activity of a God. Faith, of course, is an entirely different matter. But Paine was interested in *rational* grounds for theism, since he was appealing to those whose liberation from superstition had pushed them towards scepticism and atheism; and in the court of rationality the argument from causality to the existence of God fails. Paine's argument from design is equally flawed, and shows a lamentable ignorance of Hume's *Dialogues on Natural Religion*, which is a more than adequate counter to his rather bald assertions. This is one area in which his self-proclaimed ignorance of other writers serves him badly.

Although these flaws do not affect the force of Paine's argument against Christian orthodoxy, they do undermine his attempt to provide rational grounds for resisting atheism. Moreover, in so far as his moral and political theory depends on the premiss of a rational God commanding a rational universe, this weakness has damaging effects on the cogency of the rest of his work. To that extent we should be prepared to find fault not simply with Paine's theology, but also with his entire moral and political thought.

5 Conclusion

The grounds for natural rights

Throughout his works, Paine insists that there are certain natural rights which society and government are established to protect and which they cannot legitimately infringe. His account of these rights develops gradually, but at each stage his commitment to natural rights is unmistakable and underpins his arguments against monarchical and aristocratic rule and in favour of republican government. It seems obvious that the strength of these arguments must rely on logically prior arguments for the existence of these natural rights; for, unless he can support his claim that there are such 'indefeasible, hereditary rights of man' (I. 356), his entire political theory would seem to be undermined.

One way of avoiding this issue and its consequences is to claim, as some commentators have done, that the content of Paine's category of natural rights is entirely descriptive—that is, that it is non-normative. This requires that we interpret his claim that 'Natural rights are those which appertain to man in right of his existence' as meaning that what it is to have a natural right to x, is to have the power to x in the state of nature. But this reading is not at all plausible. It would give us a Hobbesian, not a Lockian, account of natural rights, which is entirely out of character with the rest of Paine's work. It would ignore the fact that the concept of civil rights depends on the existence of natural rights which are not equivalent to our natural powers, and would fail to acknowledge that Paine has a category of acts which we have the power to perform in the state of nature, but not the right—for example, causing harm to others or unnecessary suffering to animals (I. 512).

Paine's account of natural rights is undoubtedly normative. Like Locke, he believed that the content of our natural rights is constrained by a set of norms which are divine in origin, even if they are also discoverable by the exercise of reason, and even if that discovery is part of a long-term historical process which has culminated in the American and French revolutions. Moreover, it is because their content is sanctioned by both God and reason that they have moral weight and can be used to ground claims that society and government have a moral duty to respect them.

However, as we have seen, while assertions that these rights come from the hand of God may be rhetorically effective, their underpinnings in Paine's account are weak. His negative arguments against Christianity deprive him of the advantage, which Locke had, of revelation as a source of support; while his positive creed of rational deism does not bear much scrutiny. Faced with this difficulty, we can either agree to consign his work to the status of a curiosity from an earlier, less sceptical age, or we can reopen the issue of the dependence of his political theory on his theology and see if there is a way to salvage the thrust of the politics while abandoning its ostensible ground. This latter option has possibilities, as we can see if we refer back to Paine's attack on Burke.

Paine succeeds against Burke by reaching out to an audience previously excluded from political debate and political participation—those whom Burke demeans by his suggestion that Providence dooms them to live on trust. By treating the members of his audience as independent, rational agents capable of autonomous reflection and decision, he throws into question the legitimacy of the existing regime. Paine challenges Burke, less by his direct appeals to natural rights than by addressing his readers as equals, thereby conferring on them citizenship in the republic of political discourse. This citizenship carries with it all the essential elements of Paine's more abstract claims for natural rights: by attempting to persuade his readers of the truth of his claims, he recognizes their natural right to judge for themselves; and in arguing about the practical organization of society and government, he invites his readers to participate in a collective process the outcome of which is determined by majority opinion. By thrusting his work 'into the hands of all persons in this country, of subjects of every description', by obtruding and forcing his work 'upon that part of the public whose minds cannot be supposed to be conversant with subjects of this sort', and by addressing himself to 'the ignorant, to the credulous, to the desperate', Paine brought this citizenship to the lower orders of eighteenth-century Britain. The reason why his writing was so damaging to the status quo was simply that he wrote in a manner accessible to all, and in a such a way that his readers could not fail to recognize their right to judge. (Quotations are from the Attorney General's speech summing up the case against Paine's *Rights of Man*, Part Two (ST 381–3).)

However, the republic of political discourse to which Paine's audience is admitted is subject to certain basic norms which must be observed: reason is the basic tool of inquiry, evidence provides the fundamental data, and truth is the goal to be pursued. Force and fraud violate participants' membership rights because they transgress rational norms for achieving consensus. Political debate is fully intelligible only when seen as an activity which seeks agreement between participants by rational means. It follows that all rational beings implicated in the outcome of the activity have a right to participate, and that this right entails a duty to abide by canons of rationality. A sophisticated version of this view has been advanced recently by Jürgen Habermas, but there is no need to explore his view here. What is important to recognize here is that Paine does not need to rely on theology to support his claims that people have certain natural rights. These can be grounded more securely by shifting our focus of attention from what he actually says to the practical force and intent of his writing. It is here that he demonstrates his commitment to the regulative ideal of rational debate among equals orientated to the pursuit of truth. This ideal is itself intelligible only if those capable of participating have an indefeasible right to do so—no logically prior argument justifying this right is required. Although we may not be persuaded by Paine's late enlightenment optimism and rationalism, we can reject his orientation to truth (which grounds his natural rights claims) only by embracing a scepticism which denies that consensus on deliberative norms can be achieved without coercion and manipulation. This is a high price to pay.

Recent commentators on Paine have rightly emphasized the way in which his rough grammar, plain diction, and unpretentious prose were 'designed to hold the attention, and secure the trust of an audience which was accustomed to being governed but not to being written for' (MB 109). While their analysis of Paine's style and how it contributes to his goals has added considerably to our appreciation of his achievement, there is also a less positive side to it.

Paine's ability to communicate with a wide public had radical implications for the traditional forms of legitimation used by the State. But this is not because he created an authentic, radical, democratic prose. His prose style is a necessary, but not a sufficient, condition for his success. It is necessary because it enabled him to tap an audience which would have remained inaccessible had he written in accordance with prevailing standards of literary merit. But it was precisely because this audience was excluded from political discourse and activity in the late eighteenth century that his works had a radical impact. For, once this audience had been reached, it immediately became the target of conservative, evangelical, and nationalist propaganda which sought to resecure its allegiance to the State. Paine not only forced the patrician State to find new techniques of legitimation; he also (unintentionally) showed how legitimacy could be won—namely, by replicating his style and circulation, while peddling a very different set of creeds. During 1795 and 1796 the Government and loyalist associations provided funding for the printing and distribution of some two million copies of Hannah More's *Cheap Repository Tracts*, which sold for a penny and instructed the poor to submit to their 'fruitful penitence', to render unto Caesar his due, to fear God, and to honour the king. In a world of uncoerced communication among free, equal agents, it is unlikely that many would have found these messages persuasive; but in the world of the lower orders at the end of the eighteenth century, many doubtless found it easier to settle for More's evangelical potion than to hazard their lives and their liberty by responding to Paine. The moral of this might well be that the offer of membership in a republic of political discourse has limited appeal when acceptance involves substantial risks; or, to put it another way, prudence and the dictates of reason do not always coincide, and where they diverge, the former may easily be mistaken for the latter.

Character

This discussion of Paine's works has demonstrated that his personal habits and weaknesses did not render him incapable of writing intelligently and coherently. He thus stands vindicated against those who have attacked him with innuendo, slander, and every other tool of defamation. There remains a question of Paine's integrity as an author, however. Works such as Howard Fast's novel *Citizen Tom Paine* and, particularly, Paul Foster's play *Tom Paine* have claimed to find beneath Paine's rationalism a variety of psychological complexes and torments, and have used these to explain both his purportedly aberrant personal and social behaviour and his attitude towards his social 'superiors'. While some of this work is entertaining enough, little is persuasive. For the most part it weaves its psychological strait-jacket from 'evidence' found in the more disreputable biographical works on Paine. Consequently, there is much drinking and carousing, a good deal of swearing (which is completely, inappropriate, since Paine would leave the room if discussion degenerated into bawdy stories, apparently), some suggestion that he had recourse to prostitutes (and some that he was impotent), and frequent suggestions that he had a deeply ambivalent attitude to parental, and so to governmental, authority. None of this is very enlightening, and some of it actively inhibits understanding. Doubtless a number of factors led Paine to follow his revolutionary calling; but there is no reason to think that he did so entirely at the behest of some deep underlying psychological disturbance (unless we are so reductivist that we see all revolutionaries as deeply disturbed). Paine regarded the system of government he attacked as inherently unjust; he believed he had good grounds for this view (as indeed he did); and by native wit, ability, and a host of fortuitous circumstances which brought him to Philadelphia at the beginning of the American Revolution he devised a means of communicating his sense of injustice in a way that thousands of his contemporaries found compelling. He also tried to convey his convictions in a way which would give his readers grounds for sharing them. Indeed, perhaps the single most important reason why his work has survived, is still read, and still affects readers is that beneath the surface rhythms of his style, his clear conviction and dedication to the task of bringing contemporary politics to trial in the court of reason can be recognized. This commitment is also apparent in what some have seen as his less endearing traits. Some of his contemporaries, notably Gouverneur Morris, but also others of a similarly elevated socio-economic status, derided Paine for his lack of gentility and accused him of colossal egoism and arrogance. But these are not the characteristics we find in his correspondence or in the accounts of other contemporaries who were less outraged by an artisan coming to play a significant role in national and international affairs. This view might gain some support from the fact that Paine knew his own writings by heart, recited them in public, and repeated sections of them from one pamphlet to another, while pretending ignorance of the writings of the masters of political thought. There is also a story that he once argued that all the libraries in the world could be burnt to the ground without significant loss if they were restarted with his own works. But it remains a story from a hostile witness whom Paine may well have set out to pique. Even if true, it only confirms our view that he believed in what he was doing with utter sincerity—which is all that is necessary to defend him from his detractors.

Contribution

Paine's work owes its major principles to what we now think of as a liberal tradition of thought. That tradition is a nineteenth-century invention, as is conservatism. The French Revolution led to a parting of the ways for what had been a loosely unified tradition. Burke brings out the conservative moment of the heritage, whereas Paine turns it into a programme for radical political change designed to bring into existence, representative democracies which would combine popular sovereignty with limited government. Paine's later writings, influenced by the success of the American Revolution, proclaim the imminent collapse of ignorance and superstition, hereditary government and the Christian Church; and they predict a future of international peace, to be achieved through the elimination of monarchs and the spread of commerce. In this latter commitment he betrays his distance from the socialism which emerged in the first part of the nineteenth century. In his later writings, he also outlines one of the first proposals for a welfare state and, perhaps more significantly, develops the requisite arguments to show why such provision, achieved through progressive taxation, is owed to the poor as a matter of justice.

These are not inconsiderable contributions to political thought; and on their basis alone he deserves a place in at least the middle ranks of political thinkers. He is someone of whom politics and history undergraduates should at least have heard, even if they never read him! But these are academic standards of evaluation, and are not necessarily appropriate. Equally, looking for writers whom Paine can be credited with influencing is not likely to be fruitful. We might do better to settle for two other grounds for assessment.

The first is to look at his personal achievement. At the age of thirty-seven he was an unemployed stay-maker and excise man; when he died he was shunned by his contemporaries. But in between he rubbed shoulders with, and often influenced, most of the outstanding Americans, Frenchmen, and Englishmen of his period. He was on close, friendly terms with two American presidents (Jefferson and Monroe), a respected acquaintance of a third (Madison), an enemy of two more (John Adams and John Quincy Adams, who responded on his father's behalf to the *Rights of Man* in the *Publicola* letters), and at first a friend but later an embittered critic of another (Washington). There is no doubt that he played a greater role than many in the American Revolution, that he was the single most influential pamphleteer in Britain in the 1790s, and that he was a significant figure in the French Revolution, even if it is doubtful that he grasped fully its dynamics. Moreover, his *Age of Reason* had a profound and long-term impact on religious debate and belief in both Britain and America. This is surely, as he might have put it, 'living to some purpose' (AA 125).

121

A second, perhaps even more important criterion for assessment is Paine's influence on ordinary people. Generations of working men and women read Paine's political and theological works, thanks to their constant reprinting on popular presses and their circulation by working men's clubs and societies. This is the audience which Paine sought to reach, and there can be little doubt that he did so decade after decade. What readers learnt from him was less a substantive doctrine of politics or religion than a sense of their right to judge for themselves, something which brought in its wake the self-reliance and self-confidence necessary to organize politically and challenge the status quo. It is more appropriate to think of Paine as a revolutionary democrat than a liberal (although many of his principles are liberal ones), because the central thrust of his work was to teach the ordinary reader and citizen to question all forms of received wisdom and to demand that his right to participate as a member of a sovereign people be met fully. Although there is much that is liberal in this demand, it is one which few nation states professing liberalism could meet without introducing extensive political and social changes; and this is as true in the twentieth century as it was in Paine's time.

As a political philosopher his status may not be as great as that of other writers, but as a committed and practising democrat it is difficult to believe that it has been equalled.

Further reading

Most of Paine's works are collected in Philip S. Foner (ed.), *The Life and Major Writings of Thomas Paine*, 2 vols. (Citadel, Secaucus, N.J., 1948). Some letters and a few pamphlets are not included. The discovery of the latter is largely attributable to A. O. Aldridge, who refers to them in both his biography of Paine, *Man of Reason* (Cresset, London, 1960), and his more recent *Thomas Paine's American Ideology* (University of Delaware Press, Associated University Presses, N.J., 1984). The better-known of Paine's works, *Common Sense* and *Rights of Man*, are readily available, having been published by Penguin, amongst others. Penguin has also brought out a valuable collection which includes the major works and some of Paine's lesser-known but important works, in *The Thomas Paine Reader*, edited by M. Foot and I. Kramnick (Harmondsworth, 1987).

The best biographies of Paine are that of Aldridge (above) and Moncur Conway's path-breaking *The Life of Thomas Paine* (1892). W. E. Woodward's *Tom Paine: America's Grandfather* (Secker and Warburg, London, 1946) is less scholarly, but more entertaining. More recent biographical work, excepting D. Hawke's *Paine* (Harper and Row, New York, 1974) is disappointing. D. Powell's *Tom Paine: The Greatest Exile* (Croom Helm, London, 1984) is an imaginative attempt to reconstruct Paine's life, but goes too far and does its subject a number of disservices. Neither *Citizen of the World* (St Martin's Press, New York, 1988), ed. Ian Dyck, nor A. J. Ayer's *Thomas Paine* (Secker and Warburg, London, 1988) do much to extend our understanding of Paine or his thought, although George Spater's chapter on 'The Legacy of Thomas Paine' in Dyck's collection is informative.

Further reading

The best work on Paine's activities in America is E. Foner's *Tom Paine and Revolutionary America* (Oxford University Press, Oxford, 1976). Aldridge's *Thomas Paine's American Ideology* is less successful than both Foner's book and his own biography, despite his impeccable scholarship. B. Bailyn's *The Ideological Origins of the American Revolution* (Belknap, Harvard University Press, Cambridge, Mass., 1967) and G. Wood's *The Creation of the American Republic 1776–1787* (Norton, New York, 1969) are essential background works, while R. Bloch's *Visionary Republic: Millennial Themes in American Thought, 1756–1800* (Cambridge University Press, Cambridge, 1985) adds an extremely important dimension to our understanding of American political thought in this period. J. G. A. Pocock's work, in particular his *The Machiavellian Moment* (Princeton University Press, Princeton, 1975), has also been extremely influential on scholars working on this period.

On Paine in England, see R. R. Fennessy, *Burke, Paine, and the Rights of Man* (M. Nijhoff, The Hague, 1963), the biographies referred to above, and for the broader context H. T. Dickinson, *British Radicalism and the French Revolution, 1789–1815* (Blackwell, Oxford, 1985); I. Christie, *Stress and Stability in Late Eighteenth-Century Britain* (Oxford University Press, Oxford, 1984); A. Goodwin, *Friends of Liberty: The English Democratic Movement in the Age of the French Revolution* (Hutchinson, London, 1979); and E. P. Thompson, *The Making of the English Working Class* (Penguin, Harmondsworth, 1968).

On Paine's style, see J. T. Boulton, *The Language of Politics in the Age of Wilkes and Burke* (Routledge and Kegan Paul, London, 1963); O. Smith, *The Politics of Language* (Oxford University Press, Oxford, 1984); and M. Butler, *Burke, Paine, Godwin and the Revolutionary Controversy* (Cambridge University Press, Cambridge, 1984).

On Paine's time in France the biographies, especially that

by Aldridge, are the best sources, although it helps to read them alongside a standard work on the French Revolution (an entity which has a short life span, and one likely to be shortened still further by the bicentennial).

There is no especially good work on Paine's theology, but the first volume of L. Stephen's *English Thought in the Eighteenth Century* (first published 1876; reprinted by Harcourt, Brace & World, Inc., London, 1962) is a good introduction to the background and includes a discussion of Paine. As a detailed account of the earlier contro-versies, however, it pales besides H. G. Reventlow's *The Authority of the Bible and the Rise of the Modern World* (SCM Press, London, 1984). J. Mackie's *The Miracle of Theism* (Oxford University Press, Oxford 1982) is also of help in evaluating the strength of Paine's arguments.

The papers given by L. Kirk, E. Royle, G. Claeys, and M. Chase, at a 1988 conference to celebrate the 250th anniversary of Paine's birth, and published in the *Bulletin of the Society for the Study of Labour History*, 52 (3), 1987, pp. 3–40, are wide ranging and provide an exemplary introduction to the voluminous journal literature on Paine.

In the text I have referred to John Rawls's work *A Theory of Justice* (Oxford University Press, Oxford, 1972) and to the work of Jürgen Habermas—for which see *Legitimation Crisis* (Heinemann, London, 1973) and *A Theory of Communicative Action*, vol. 1 (Beacon, Boston, 1984). Q. Skinner's edited collection of essays entitled *The Return of Grand Theory in the Human Sciences* (Cambridge University Press, Cambridge, 1985) contains good clear introductory essays on both Rawls (by Alan Ryan) and Habermas (by Anthony Giddens).

Index

Index